COLLECT YOUR PEARLS OF WISDOM

Effective techniques to heal
and transform your life.

D R .   O L G A   Z A B O R A

BALBOA.PRESS
A DIVISION OF HAY HOUSE

Balboa Press books may be ordered through booksellers or by contacting:

Balboa Press
A Division of Hay House
1663 Liberty Drive
Bloomington, IN 47403
www.balboapress.com
844-682-1282

Disclaimer:
Please note the information contained within this document is for educational and entertainment purposes only. Please consult a licensed professional before attempting any practices outlined in this book. This is not a therapy and not a substitute for therapy. Doing some of the exercises has the potential to be upsetting, although it is unusual. If it is psychologically upsetting to you, please call a licensed mental health professional.

Readers acknowledge that the author is not engaged in the rendering of legal, financial, medical, or professional advice. By reading this document, the reader agrees that under no circumstances is the author responsible for any losses, direct or indirect, that are incurred as a result of the use of the information contained within this document, including but not limited to errors, omissions, or inaccuracies.

Print information available on the last page.

ISBN: 979-8-7652-4385-5 (sc)
ISBN: 979-8-7652-4519-4 (hc)
ISBN: 979-8-7652-4386-2 (e)

Library of Congress Control Number: 2023913238

Balboa Press rev. date: 08/28/2023

Please scan QR code at the end of this book
to receive three free gifts from my website,
DrOlgaZabora.com:

Inner Child Meditation
The Ring of Power Training
Past Life Regression Meditation

I take opposites and conflicts
all that is contradictory
I take the diverse and varied
I take the simple and solitary
mix and merge, meld and blend
I take what is separate and create union
I bring together
what needs to be brought together
so wholeness is achieved.
—Gyhldeptis in Amy Sophia Marashinsky's *The Goddess Oracle*

Contents

Part 3: Dive Deeper into Your Subconscious Mind to Find Your Bliss and Freedom

Introduction

JOURNEY TO WHOLENESS

Welcome, my dear reader, to this adventure. I am inviting you to embark on this transformational journey with me. I am happy and honored to share these discoveries, insights, and practices that helped to heal and transform people's lives, including mine.

This book came out of witnessing the transformations of my clients over the years through clinical work, coaching, and experiencing my own transformational journey by exploring the human psyche through different techniques and practices individually and within groups. It came out from the depths of my psyche to the surface of my conscious awareness and now to the world.

My own transformative journey of profound exploration of the human psyche started a long time ago. I delved into the psychology field when I was eighteen with Freudian psychoanalysis, concentrating specifically on dream analysis. This initial step sparked a deep curiosity within me to understand the inner workings of the mind and the depth of our subconscious mind. Driven by a thirst for knowledge and personal growth, I actively engaged in Jungian workshops and seminars regularly at that time and considered a psychology degree later in life. At the same time, I was immersed in transpersonal psychology with Stan Grof's books and breathwork retreats. Through the consistent practice of Holotropic Breathwork™ (developed by Dr. Stan Grof, MD, PhD, and his wife, Kristina) I experienced profound states of consciousness and accessed a deeper layer of my own psyche.

Continuing my quest, I ventured into realms of hypnosis and Past Life Regressions, Life Between Lives regressions, peering into mysteries of our past and uncovering hidden insights that could shed light on our present lives. My exploration did not stop there, I eagerly pursued a comprehensive Jungian program, delving further into the realms of archetypes and dream analysis. I also delved into philosophical tantra, studying the profound teachings of Kashmir Shaivism with Sally Kempton. Seeking connection with ancient wisdom, I embarked on shamanic journeys, following the footsteps of Michael's Harners Foundation for three years.

To refine my understanding and deepen my ability to support others, I became a Master NLP Coach and NLP Trainer's Trainer, honing my skills in guiding individuals towards transformation and growth. I also embraced mindfulness practices, incorporating the teaching from mindfulness UCLA programs into my practice with clients and in my own life.

As I am looking back, all of my young adulthood years, I was bathed in these deep soul-searching practices. No matter where I was, I would always find them: New York, California, Hawaii, India, and more. It was my path to search for depth, wisdom, and transformation of consciousness. Much later, I realized it was my journey to the depths to retrieve pearls of wisdom, which you can read about here, and you can learn how to retrieve your own wisdom and bring transformation to your life.

I was continuously searching, diving in and out of the practices. But one event particularly clarified this and helped me to come to a turning point. When I was in my first year of Master of Clinical Psychology program, I came to Dr. Jack Kornfield for his weekend program, when he was teaching Buddhist Psychology in Los Angeles. I had a profound visual experience during his guided meditation process.

I had a vision of a cosmic midnight and a magical beach with a full moon. A woman sitting on the shore half submerged herself in the mesmerizing waters of the ocean amid a warm breeze, observing the full moon. The moon road was reflecting on the surface of the water.

The waters of the ocean were allowing the light from the moon to go deeper through the layers of water, and I started to see the light reflecting from the depths of the ocean. I realized the woman on the shore was me. I saw a magnificent light that was reflected in the depths that drew my full attention. I was curious about the light, so I dove in. Diving deeper and deeper, I finally was able to reach the floor and touched a beautiful, shining pearl at the bottom of the ocean. I felt as if I were touching something precious. I treasured the pearl as if it were something I had forgotten at some point in my life, and now I had found it again; it had revealed itself to me.

That precious pearl I was able to identify in the depths became a symbol for me, signifying that I was on the right track with my psychology field and the exploration of the human psyche. While going back from the dark blue depths of the sea with treasure in my hands, I felt much freer and more joyful. I was happy to discover it, retrieve it, and bring it to the surface. I felt I was on the right path!

This was my symbol of transformation, the preciousness of deep psychological work: going through my personal therapy, learning about the mind, the psyche, Jungian archetypes, complexes, dream analysis, and much more. The full moon in the sky and the pearl at the bottom of the sea (notice they have the same shape) became symbols of the heights and depths of the human psyche, which allow us to retrieve this beautiful, precious knowledge and live our wisdom consciously.

It became the guiding principle for me to live this wisdom as a transformative self. Diving deeper into the depths of the ocean became a metaphor for bringing up the wisdom from the depths of my being to the conscious level.

Here you can read these stories and see what resonates with you. I created the book as a collection of them to demonstrate the techniques that may bring transformation for you too. After each chapter, you will find a description and guidance of practices for your personal exploration. These stories are intended to help you transform your consciousness and inspire you to take on a transformational journey by using these techniques.

"Collecting Your Pearls of Wisdom" represents the amalgam of powerful stories and journeys that people went through, like a string of beads connected to one another. So you can read and learn from it and then practice. They are precious, valuable experiences that can be told to others so they can blaze their trails as well, help to transform human consciousness, learn from the examples, learn about their power. Identify the stories that resonate with you and the wisdom you gain from them. Ask yourself: What are the learnings you got as a result of them, and how can you be refined and redefined as a result of these challenges? Learning and valuing these experiences will help all of us to elevate our human condition and heal our hearts and wounds so we can connect through love, not through pain.

One of the objectives of this book is to inspire you to go through your own journey—to dive into your depths, retrieve your unique pearls, collect them, and maybe share them to inspire others.

Also, reading the stories will entertain you. They will serve as examples to show you that you can heal too, as others have, and to bring curiosity and courage to explore deeper your being.

The other goals are to teach; guide you through difficulties; create insights and courage to practice; and help you to step forward on this difficult yet gratifying journey with winning results that bring you to wholeness, greater self-awareness, love, and compassion for yourself and others and allow you to embody your new insights.

Healing and Wholeness

Did you ever ask yourself what healing is? Healing is to become whole. This collection of stories may help you to identify which part of you needs or wants to be healed or is ready to be healed and integrated into wholeness. When you realize that wounded parts of yourself are taking space within you and recognize that healing or change needs to take place, you will start your process, and it will happen only when you are ready. That's why you are reading this book now.

Once those parts are healed and integrated, you now have space available for loving and healthy connections, and you can relate to others through love, not through pain. Instead of acting out the wounds with others in an unconscious attempt to repair dysfunctional patterns, you have an opportunity to work through them and heal and, thus, can relate to others from a balanced state of love and care.

My intense Doctoral Clinical Psychology training, Neuro-Linguistic Programming coaching program, and years of other holistic modalities gave me an opportunity to draw from both therapeutic and coaching perspectives, so I can share an integrative approach to healing and transformation. Out of all the stories, you can choose what's best for you and what resonates with you the most. Take the best, and bless the rest! Follow the instructions at the end of each chapter, and use the technique for at least twenty-one days or even forty days to practice to live your new habits, skills, behaviors, choices, and new version of yourself.

Pay special attention when you decide to explore the wounds, because doing so may touch painful states, and it's not always easy. Get help when needed. We have homeostasis, and when things start to shift, most people have resistance to change. We are all creatures of habit; thus, be patient, and be gentle with yourself. Give yourself appreciation, acknowledgment, and rewards for doing this work.

These are not all the possible techniques that exist, but they are impactful examples showing that transformation is possible. Always find what works for you. You may choose to find the right therapist, coach, or other guide who will hold your hand through this transformational process.

Most people see these stories as valuable examples of people going through the challenges and transformational process. It's a mesmerizing collection of stories, like a tapestry of life with its ups and downs, leaving you with certainty that healing is possible.

Transformational Process

When you ask yourself, "What is transformation?" what comes to mind?

Transformation occurs once we recognize that something is not working anymore and needs to be rearranged, so we unpack and change it and then put it into a new shape or form. Most people want to have transformation one way or another; either they have a desire for something they want in life, or they want to get rid of something, such as pain, unhappiness, or some kind of uncomfortable state or condition.

Sometimes being too comfortable in life may not bring the necessity to change, because we feel good about where we are in life. But on the other hand, to transform and adapt to new conditions in life is a result of the loss of a loved one, a sudden diagnosis, moving to a different city, job loss, or divorce. Can you think about a time in your life when you wanted or needed to change? How did you go through this transitional time?

This book is about transformation. It's about collecting your lessons, your wisdom, and making your transformational journey yours. Make it unique; make it special, as you are. Transformation may happen on different levels by using different techniques for different needs. I'm sharing this map so you will know what to take with you on your journey. It is like packing your backpack with basic stuff you will need to start your journey, travel, or hike, and I provide the map so you can find your own way through it.

How do we go through this transformation?

Historically, transformation has been described in alchemical literature, when alchemists were transforming lead to gold. In this book, we are going to talk about transformation of the psyche and mind—symbolic transformation.

The transformational process described in alchemy comes in three stages. Translating from Latin, the stages are *nigredo* (blackening), *albedo* (whitening), and *rubedo* (reddening).

The first stage implies that we face a condition that no longer serves us. It is painful or unbearable. We are hitting the ground (*prima materia*), where we have to face our fears and confusion and meet the shadow. In the movies, we see similar fabulae in which a hero is faced with difficulties and challenges in life. He has to move through a transformational journey in order to overcome the challenges or win the battle. It's called a heroic journey. In mythological terms, we call it the "descent" that makes us face our pain, fears, demons, or shadow, as it is called in Jungian therapy. This stage is called nigredo, or blackening.

Nigredo involves entering the unknown. The old self's ego has to tolerate feeling lost, and energy goes into the depths. It includes pain, confusion, or a feeling of stuckness. Here happens the recognition for a need to change.

Then the person will start looking for a solution and move from nigredo to the albedo stage. Albedo, or whitening, represents "cleaning or doing the laundry," which is equal to doing the internal work, dealing with shadow material. During this process, we often need a guide who will help us go through this process. Once the internal work is done and insights and learnings are retrieved, then the person experiences a sense of completion, peace, and harmony. The work is done.

The next stage is called rubedo, or reddening, and it involves integrating knowledge and new qualities into everyday life. It's a new union: you and your larger personality now are part of the new life, bringing a new point of view into daily life, a new way of living, loving, and relating. During this stage of transformation, a person learns how to live the updated, upgraded conditions. I describe this process in chapter 11, "Understand the Change (Universal Model of Change)," and chapter 12, "Choosing and Living Your New You." This book offers you a journey in three stages as well. So you know it is possible to transform, there is a beginning and end of this transformational journey, and we usually go through transformational journeys during life not once. The whole process of life is a transformational journey, isn't it?

Structure of the Book

In part 1, you will find examples through which you can work with your biographical material and family of origin as well, retrieving your joy and creativity by restoring the relationship with your precious part of you: Inner Child, touching upon your ancestors who brought you life through previous generations.

You can recognize the need for change and make your first steps toward your whitening process, the inner process of transformation.

The second part will allow you to reconnect with yourself and find yourself through your breath and heartbeat observation meditations. Then you will be able to refine your mind and learn how to dive deeper into your subconscious mind through visualization, creating new healthy rituals and learning about your mindset, your resources, and new strategies that will help you to manifest the life you want. It is a continuation of the transformation. You will read stories from people's lives in which you can see what can be done to live new insights. They live their power and their new best version of themselves, manifest their dreams, and choose the best of themselves every day by making new choices and practicing new desired behaviors.

Part 3 offers you examples that show you the depth you can achieve on your journey. The mesmerizing highs and lows of transformational journeys are evident through magnificent stories involving the healing power of dreams, regressive hypnosis into past lives, and examples of working on a transpersonal level, which Holotropic Breathwork™ offers you. Also, you will be able to witness diving deeper into your depth of psyche, finding your way back from the immersion to the depths of your being and soul story. At the end of this part, you will discover an integration chapter that teaches you how to bring changes into your everyday life, living with an expanded state of consciousness, new resources and insights and how to embody them.

How to Use This Book

First of all, you may ask, "Why stories?" We all have heard bedtime stories, fairy tales, and stories in Hollywood movies. We are all mesmerized by heroic journeys and transformations, aren't we? Our ancestors were as well.

Since ancient times, humans have learned from storytelling, transferring wisdom and valuable experience from generation to generation through folklore, fairy tales, and myths. Listeners are able to imagine the journey and its transformation to encode in their catalog of experiences, with a successful ending and the ability to overcome challenges or difficulties in their lives. I chose carefully the transformational stories. Each story is like a minijourney of a hero and it has its transformative power. You too can do it! I find that these techniques help us learn our lessons on our healing journey and discover unconditional love and support. I call them pearls of wisdom in your sacred box. Learn from them, treasure them, and live your joyous life.

It is an invitation to explore your deeper self, and your relationships. After each chapter, you will find exercises. If you are inspired by them, practice. Choose the story that resonates with you, and reflect on it. Do the exercises and journal. If a story resonates with you or you've experienced something similar, use this opportunity to write down your wisdom or lessons so you can come back at a later time to track the progress you have made. Again, take the best, and bless the rest!

Meet yourself where you are, and work with what you are ready to process. Move toward what you want and how you want to be every day step by step, but be consistent. Integrate it into your life by choosing a new you every day. Share your success with your loved ones so they can heal too.

During the process of retrieving your unique pearls, you may choose to create your necklace or bracelet as a symbol of transformation that is unique to your being, your psyche, your own story, and your own precious jewelry box for your soul. Value it, cherish it, and shine your light for others.

A word of caution: know yourself and your capabilities. If it is too raw and too emotional, find the right therapist or support group to guide you and hold your hand during this process, which may not always be easy. I offer online classes with a live Q&A group and practice these techniques. You may find it on my website, DrOlgaZabora.com, with three gifts: two meditations and the Ring of Power training. You will find a QR code for it at the end of the book.

Courage needs to be present to dive into the depths of your being, but the rewards are magnificent. Make sure you give yourself time to integrate your experiences and learn how to live your new version of yourself to solidify your new habits, beliefs, and behaviors.

Stay tuned: a deck of cards complementary to this book, with self-care practices, is planned to be published in 2023. The cards will serve you as a reminder of your progress and will help you to practice daily. You may choose to pick one or two at a time, stick with them, and practice for twenty-one days, or you may draw a new card every day to practice only that day.

Enjoy reading and practicing the exercises, and keep your playful spirit during the process. The universe has a sense of humor. I'm wishing you a transformative and healing journey!

Part 1

HEAL YOUR FAMILY WOUNDS AND CONNECTING TO ANCESTORS

This is dedicated to my father, my mother,
all of our fathers and mothers,
and all of us as children of our ancestors, with gratitude for our lives
and the opportunity to heal and learn from our family wounds.
May we collect our pearls of wisdom and
restore the flow of energy and love between generations.

Part 1 contains episodes of healing my family wounds that I had to revisit myself and examples from my clients as well, who shared with me their processes of growth, wisdom, and healing they were able to obtain through transformational work. Here you will dive into biographical material and will be able to witness and practice connection to your ancestors as well, the ones who came before you.

In chapter 1 and chapter 2, you will read about the main relationships in childhood, primarily the mother and father. Most of the time, we have wounds started from our family of origin. Read the examples, and reflect on how they're related to your own life.

Chapter 3 talks about the first trauma we get, which is called the birth trauma. You may inquire and journal on your own birth conditions.

In chapter 4, you will dive into the process of recovering the Inner Child, the creative part of us. Most of the time, it is a long-forgotten part that has been disowned. You will have a chance to witness how to dust it off, revive this treasure, and integrate it back to create wholeness.

Also, you will find ancestral healing stories here as well. There is a chance to get to know your family history, patterns, and how you are like your parents and grandparents. Treasure and honor your ancestors and their life stories, and learn from them. This is intended to help you become aware of the patterns of pain that can be transformed and transcended. Re-membering (*re-* meaning to bring them back as members of the system) your family members can be done through Family Constellation modality, which is described in chapter 5.

According to the transformational alchemical process, we first recognize the pain or need for change, and then we start looking for solutions. It's the beginning of the whitening stage of starting to do the "internal laundry," cleaning the slate.

The heart of man is very much like the sea,
it has its storms, it has its tides and in its depths,
it has its pearls too.
—Vincent van Gogh

Chapter I

FATHER: THE HEALING POWER OF A LETTER

During a sunny spring day in Los Angeles, I woke up excited—mainly because I was scheduled for a reading with my longtime astrologist, Glenn. My usual readings were about my chart, transits, soul mission, and so on. This time, I decided to try something different and exceptional, and thus, I could barely wait until the time came for the session. I counted the minutes until I heard the phone ring. When it did, I asked Glenn to do a reading about my father, who'd passed away fifteen years earlier from a heart attack in his sleep, when he was almost forty-five years old. I had that particular need for this type of consultation because I always had space in my heart, a hole—a wound, you could call it—of missing him, and my expectation of this session was to create a deeper connection and feel his presence in my life through this reading.

I went through my healing journey using different kinds of therapeutic modalities to fill this gap of missing my father. Yet I felt something was still not there in my life. I'm sure many can relate to the father's wound, one way or another. Usually, the father is the first man in a woman's life. He gives the seed to her mother, who creates and gives birth to a baby. Mother and father are symbolically portrayed in fairy tales as a queen and a king. They are the first woman and man in a child's world, the role models. When the positive parent archetypes are playing out in a person's life, the mother is a fairy who magically creates food, and the father is the hero.

I remembered my father as a hero. I always remembered him as a big, strong man with a full beard after spending a few months in the wild. He was a geologist, so I saw him every six months of the year, due to his work. But when he returned, he would bring bags full of goodies, including wild strawberries he preserved in the wilderness, bags full of pine nuts, and so much love.

He was *my hero*. When I was six and a half years old, my friend and I got stuck in my building's elevator. We started to panic and scream after the emergency button was silent, and we realized nobody was going to rescue us. My father heard us screaming, ran out of the apartment, and saw that the elevator door was open about four inches and stuck. I saw him quickly rush to push the doors with his strong torso and move them inch by inch. He did not know if we were injured or not, so he pushed as hard as he could and as quickly as possible. I saw how his back was sweating and bruised, with blood appearing on his skin. Finally, magically, the doors opened, and we were freed and saved from our cage. Later that evening, my whole family and many of our neighbors talked about my father as a hero saving us. I saw how my mom put ointment on the scratches and bruises on his shoulders, and I felt so much love and gratitude toward him. Knowing I was safe and loved, I went to bed. It was like being wrapped in loving, strong arms, being protected, happy, and proud of my father as a hero.

During the astrology reading, this story was told to remember and honor my father and his energy, to restore and fill in my bottomless hole of missing him in my life. Glenn would agree to do this reading with a disclaimer: I was a longtime professional client and had studied astrology before, so we would be on the same page. We looked at the sun and the moon in both my father's and my charts, how they were connected, and how other planets would have played out in our lives if he were alive and if we had our relationship right now, including what discussions we might have had. The ninety-minute astrology session flew by. At the end, I felt that it was still insufficient and that something was still missing. Glenn suggested I write a letter to my father. I followed his advice.

That evening, I created the sacred space: I turned off my cell phone, lit a candle, said blessings, and set my healing intention. I took out the pictures of my father and me together, especially memorable ones taken when we were going on trips, such as when he would take me to the zoo as a toddler. I took out a stack of paper and started to write the letter. I wrote while laughing and crying, telling him how much I missed him and how much I loved him. I felt grief and loss, love, and gratitude. I did this sacred practice for forty days.

As you may know, forty days is a holy number in different religions and cultures where prayers are said, mantras are chanted, and fasting occurs. Transformation happens when a person is taking on austerities—spiritual practice, or sadhana, that purifies the body and mind of a yogi. I did this sacred practice every day until that final day when my tears dried out, and my heart was filled with light, love, and peace. I felt the closure I needed. I put away our pictures, burned all the letters, let the smoke disappear into the night air and merge with the father sky, and went to bed feeling safe and secure, as if I were that little six-and-a-half-year-old girl saved by her hero father. Synchronistically, that fortieth day fell on my father's birthday—the day when he would have had his sixtieth birthday.

The following day was a Sunday, and I drove on the Pacific Coast Highway, or the PCH, toward Capistrano Beach, enjoying the ocean view on one side and the mountains on the other side of the freeway. On my route, I saw a crystal shop and decided to stop by. The moment I stepped into the store, the woman working there asked if I would like to take a picture of my aura—modern computerized Kirlian technology. I had not done it for a couple of years, so I decided I would.

A woman ushered me into a small room with a heavy curtain instead of a door. I saw a computer monitor and palm-shaped sensor. The moment I put my palm on the sensor, the woman looked at me, shocked, and asked, "Did somebody die recently in your family?"

I said immediately, "No, not that I am aware of." However, I started to think, and then I questioned her about why she'd asked.

She pointed to the top of the picture, where I saw a white light and a wing shape. She said, "Angels. Here they are."

I started to wail and told her about my practice of writing the healing letter to my father for the last forty days and said I had finished it on his birthday. She looked at me with love and inspiration as she saw the angels around me and said, "Here he is. He is here with you!"

I was in a trancelike state. When I opened the curtain, going back to the main room, the first thing I saw was that a clay medallion was among the other crystals on the table. The blue color was like the Pacific Ocean, with a white angel on it. I stretched my hand toward it, gently held it in my hand, and then flipped it and read, "I am blessed."

I paid for the aura picture, the medallion, and a couple of candles and left the crystal shop. I sat in my car, holding the medallion and the photo with white angel wings on top of my head. I felt how my tears of joy, grace, and unconditional love streamed down my face. I felt truly blessed, connected, and loved. I knew he was there with me, protecting me. He protected me when he was alive with his arms and now with his angel wings. While looking at the medallion, I whispered, "Thank you, Dad. I love you too."

I felt complete and confirmed by the power of healing, the letter writing, and the synchronicities, which were always guiding me on my life path and healing journey.

When I share this magnificent story with my clients or anybody else, they incorporate the letter-writing technique into their healing journeys. They return to me and report long-lasting healing results, restorative power, love, fulfillment, and grace or closure while grieving their loved ones, as I had. As a result of this process, I witnessed the life flow restored in people, wisdom thrived, and the eyes were full of life force and gratitude for the love and relationships they had.

The letter-writing practice is widely used in many healing modalities. In my practice, I have witnessed many stories from my clients of the father's wound, which can present itself as an absent father, unavailable father, or other. It gave me additional reassurance to share the story about the healing power of writing a letter. But if people went through trauma in their lives, they need to have assistance with a mental health professional who is trained in healing the trauma.

This practice can be done in many different ways. You can write this letter to a loved one, relative, family member, or friend, deceased or alive. Make sure you do not send it to the person, and utilize it the safest way possible. It's not about the person reading your letter; it's about you healing, discharging your negative emotions and energy, or getting closure.

As a variation of this practice, you may write to yourself in the future, when the problem is already solved or the challenge is overcome. In this case, you may save this letter for the future for yourself, so you can read it later on, like pacing yourself in the future. You may write a gratitude letter to yourself for doing the job or encourage yourself to start the work on your healing journey.

Interestingly enough, for writers, Kelly Notaras recommends writing a letter to yourself before you finish a book. Once the book is written and published, then you can read that letter from your past self. Write it as if you were a grateful reader of your own book. What an amazing practice.

I invite you to be curious about what may come from this practice. Keep a journal, and keep track of your progress so you may share with others if you choose to. Know that your story can be support, light, and encouragement for others.

Transformational Practices

Technique

Write a letter to someone you have a challenging or difficult relationship with, or write a letter to a loved one who is no longer with you. Do not send it. Write as many times as you need to discharge and transform your energy.

My Insights

What did I learn from the story and this exercise? What are my lessons, my pearls of wisdom, I will collect here?

_____

_____

_____

_____

_____

_____

_____

_____

_____

_____

What are my aha moments?

_____

_____

_____

_____

_____

_____

_____

_____

_____

_____

_____

_____

_____

_____

_____

_____

_____

What will I do differently next time?

_____

_____

_____

_____

_____

_____

_____

_____

_____

_____

_____

_____

_____

_____

_____

_____

A pearl is a beautiful thing
that is produced by an injured life.
If we had not been wounded,
if we had not been injured,
then we will not produce the pearl.
—Stephan Hoeller

Chapter 2

MOTHER: SACRED RETURN TO DIVINE MOTHER

Transformation can start from having a desired change or a necessity that will make us change direction in our lives, such as a hit from life: a car accident, divorce, a sudden loss, a health diagnosis, and so on. Most of the time, we rarely seek transformation on our own. Instead, we typically get to push on to a new level of development by being forced to heal our wounds. We have a choice to hold on to the wound, carry it all our lives, and transfer the destructive or unsuccessful habitual pattern onto the next generation. Or you can face the challenge, your shadow; heal your wound; and be more present in your and your loved ones' lives. It's your choice. The story about my car accident illustrates that necessity made me dive deeper into healing and transformation. You may recall any of your stories as well when you've had any push or hit from life that created a necessity for changes in your life.

It was a beautiful, charming, sunny day in Los Angeles, California, in mid-December. I left the beauty salon, feeling all made up and pretty with my hair and nails done. I felt on top of the world. I started my car, and just as I was about to change lanes at just five miles per hour, I felt a significant impact from the left side. *Boom!* I hit the left side of my head against the metallic side of my car, and then I felt shock, confusion, disorientation, and dizziness.

At that moment, I did not realize it was a concussion. I had never had head trauma before. But that hit happened to me, prompting and reminding me that it was another layer to heal to continue my path of healing my mother's wound and my birth trauma triggered by a car accident.

That day, my life path turned in a different direction, toward a healing journey to my deeper self. Years before this car accident, when I graduated from psychology school, I felt pretty good after finishing the individual therapy course (that is necessary to get a diploma) and was sure I was done by then, but this car accident made me work even harder than before.

I hit the left side of my brain, which controls the right side of the body (the masculine) and is associated with logic, reasoning, analyzing information, and computation skills. The right brain is associated with abstract meaning, intuition, emotion, music, and art and governs the left side of the body (the feminine). I was forced to stop my active "male way" of living, my animus (masculine) flow of life focused on achieving goals and being productive ("Go, go, go. Do, do, do"), to slow down and uncover more of my anima (feminine) qualities ("Just be"). Instead of dismissing this part of life, I embraced it, and it allowed me to create wholeness in my being, integrating and balancing male and female polarities.

The concussion I got from that accident steered me from my successful private practice as a highly trained psychologist toward slowing down in life and releasing my caseload until I could perform again, due to short-term memory issues and other concussion symptoms, which took about six months to heal.

Usually, I actively participate in life. But right after the accident, I had to stay still for three weeks because every step or bend made the blood flow toward my head; nausea, headache, and dizziness would immediately flood me. So from stillness, my journey began.

Of course, my regular yoga practice and hiking were paused, which made me feel even worse, but I knew I had to stay still and heal from the inside. Everything paused in all areas of my life. I felt like a baby in this regressed state, learning about the world around me. Everything was new, but the difference was that being professional brought anxiety about returning to work and being as efficient as I used to be. Would I be able to lead my exciting life as a psychologist and perform again? Would I be able to "survive"? It was like how a baby feels anxiety and fear at being removed from its mother, the source of life and resources. That situation triggered my mother's wound, even though I had worked on my relationship with my mother before. I took care of my mother and my family for most of my adult years. Now I was in a "regressed" state, thus the care and healing I needed first. And I needed to reinvent myself. First things first: I had to take care of myself. Being forced by an accident, I learned a lot about self-care and prioritizing yourself as an act of self-love. Otherwise, I would have continued to give myself to others to the point of exhaustion. Now, having this wisdom and hard-learned experience, I prompt my clients to learn healthy boundaries and their needs and wants to make progress on individuation and healthy relationships with themselves and others.

As I mentioned before, it was a challenging journey at first. When I could walk without nausea and dizziness, I started to search for solutions: the best supplements to restore memory and appointments with different healers and practitioners. Physical therapies would not give me my desired result: I wanted to return to where I had been before, where I used to function, where I had my sweet spot in life, where I felt most comfortable in my body, my mind, and my professional activity. The worst thing for me was realizing that there was no way back! The world was no longer the same.

My memory would not work as it had before. Before, I could have a whole day full of sessions with clients, and the next day, I could write my notes word by word about what had happened during the therapy sessions. Not anymore.

I had to find my way. Embarrassingly, I would go to the store to buy one thing and then find myself at home with many other things I never intended to buy and not the one I needed.

Every evening, before going to sleep, I would ask myself, "Where is my usual, comfortable me? Who am I now?" and I would continue to meditate.

Before returning to my healing profession, I needed to find healing for myself. I had to dive much deeper into exploration of the roles we play in our lives as mothers, sisters, daughters, healers, therapists, and others.

We are more than the roles we play in life. The more I actively searched for healing and answers, the more counterproductive it became. Usually, Holotropic Breathwork™ works to release tension in the body or create more profound healing and connection to my inner self. However, not this time around. I could not strain myself, nor would yoga asanas or any bending positions work, which made me feel worse than ever.

Stillness, simplicity, and ease were my best allies at that time to become aware of my basic needs and the self-love I needed. It was an excellent lesson for me because I can now teach my female clients self-love and self-care practices, balance between masculine and feminine energies, lifestyle, and well-being at my retreats and breakthrough coaching transformational programs, so they can integrate that knowledge into their lives.

After six months of struggling, I suddenly remembered that a few months before my car accident and the concussion, I had gone to a Vipassana meditation course for ten days. I again went through this sacred stillness that resides inside me. With Vipassana meditation, you meditate for up to sixteen hours a day, silently—no writing, phone, internet, or TV distractions, just you and forty other women and men going through a silent journey that Buddha took. We were given a schedule to wake up at four thirty in the morning and meditate in our rooms until the gong called us for a nourishing vegetarian breakfast at eight, cooked in silence by assistants who went through the practice themselves. On the last day, we had metta meditation to bless everyone and everything—all living beings, including ourselves. It was a rejuvenating and beautiful experience. But I did not know that I was there for a treat. My joy and happiness were yet to come.

On my way back from the meditation center, I realized my memory had come back! Magically. Oh my God! I was back. My memory was back. I was back to myself. I could feel the freedom to express myself fully and creatively with full power and life force. I touched my inner self and connected to the divine part in all of us. I was almost dancing in my car with tears of joy, gratitude, and grace! "I am back! I am back to myself!" I yelled happily. But I would never be the same and never forget that healing journey, and I would always honor my inner sacred self. I felt I was held by the whole universe, by the Divine Mother. The grace would come my way so that the healing and unconditional love would pour from all the corners of the universe, from every rock, tree, and person. Oh, Divine Mother, the nature of the intelligence inside us. Deep gratitude and love for healing made me even more refined, redefined, deep, and profound. I drove in this expanded state for a while. I felt infinite possibilities being dissolved in Mother Goddess's energy—Bhuvaneshwari, one of those goddesses in Indian tradition who worships the Divine Mother in her different faces and forms.

Bhuvaneshwari, in Sanskrit, means "She embraces the cosmos in her whole being." She represents the eternal mother energy as the space that contains all that is. Her essence feels like a vast cosmic womb filled with loving, subtle mother energy. Her space allows you to float in her as in the cosmic ocean, as in a human mother's womb. That was how I felt in having my refined identity back. I was not defined by my wound anymore. I was redefined!

I have been seen and held by a loving presence, a compassionate witness of the Divine Mother.

According to Indian tradition, as a cosmic child, you can offer her all your anxiety and fear or whatever no longer serves you or needs healing. She will take it in, transform it, and return it back to you in the energy of peace. Her spaciousness allows her to dissolve everything that needs to be healed. I meditated on her a lot and released my leftover anxiety and fear back to the Divine Mother, Bhuvaneshwari, feeling totally held and embraced in this protective energy. I was back to loving flow again! It was a miracle of meditation. After that experience and journey, I learned even more the depth of presence of a compassionate witness as I witnessed people's healing journeys the same way I was witnessed by this divine presence during these expanded meditative states.

During this healing process, I was collecting my pearls of wisdom. I had to learn to be still and take care of my body in need, learning self-love and prioritizing. A regular car accident was transformed into a sacred journey to my depths. When we transcend our wounds and learn from them, we step into the wounded-healer archetype, who can bring wisdom and healing to others as well. It's your choice.

Transformational Practices

Technique

You may already know about this type of meditation; if not, then you may google "Vipassana meditation" or any other meditation practice of your choice. I offer free guided meditations on my website (scan QR Code at the end of the book).

My Insights

What did I learn from the story and this exercise? What are my lessons, my pearls of wisdom, I will collect here?

_____

_____

_____

_____

_____

_____

_____

_____

_____

What are my aha moments?

_____

_____

_____

_____

_____

_____

_____

_____

_____

_____

_____

_____

_____

_____

_____

_____

What will I do differently next time?

_____

_____

_____

_____

_____

_____

_____

_____

_____

_____

_____

_____

_____

_____

_____

_____

When we heal birth,
We heal the Earth.
—Jeannine Parvati Baker

Chapter 3

CHILD: DEALING WITH TRIGGERED BIRTH TRAUMA

The car accident and concussion described in the previous chapter also triggered my birth trauma, not only working with my mother's relationship. It is now widely known that the conditions at birth and the way we are born affect us on a deep level upon our entrance to this world. Dr. Stan Grof, MD, PhD, extensively writes about the birth trauma that people go through during labor. He explains four stages of labor and names them the Four Basic Perinatal Matrices (BPM). A difficult birth and any complications, such as bridge, an umbilical cord around the neck, or a baby taken out with forceps or by C-section, have an impact on a baby physically and psychologically (for more information, see the resources).

Even though I had already worked through this trauma and experienced rebirth with Holotropic Breathwork™ (developed by Dr. Stan Grof and his wife, Kristina) many years earlier and consistent exploration of Family Constellations therapy (developed by Bert Hellinger, a German psychotherapist), I still had to revisit my birth conditions again. It's like peeling an onion, going deep with each layer you have to peel.

As I mentioned earlier, the accident influenced me to make unusual food choices, such as milk cravings. I noticed that when I went to the grocery store, I would have an intense craving for whipped cream or milk. I'd never had such a strong desire to drink milk. And guess what:

when picking up the next bottle of milk, I realized that I needed to soothe myself like a baby.

After a few days of drinking milk, I developed an allergic reaction—a skin rash around my mouth and cheeks. It looked terrifying: redness, scabs around my mouth and nose, and peeling skin. I had not had skin rashes or allergies before, and I was devastated. But I knew I had to go through my healing journey and learn from it.

Family Constellation and Realigning of Energy Flow between Generations

I scheduled a Family Constellations therapy session again. You may have heard about Family Constellations or Systemic Constellations modality, which was created by Bert Hellinger, a German psychotherapist. He was traveling to Africa as a missionary and learned the shamanic technique from the tribes. They taught him how to work and align energy with ancestors. He was able to bring wisdom to the Western world regarding how to restore the flow of love between generations so the next generation will live their lives without the burden of the previous one. He was taught how not to take on their pain but to give back the "pain" as an honorable lesson they needed to learn themselves, honor the journey of previous generations, untie the knots, release the stuck energy to use for their own life achievements, and let it flow toward future generations.

We, out of love, may take on the pain of previous generations out of gratitude in exchange for our lives. It is the main idea in this therapeutic modality. During that session, I was able to release the fear that my mother was experiencing during labor and pregnancy. I was taking on her fears by then.

I was able to turn back to my mom, honor her journey, and give her the opportunity to live her lesson; otherwise, I would stand in the spot for her as a parent, as a "big one," and it creates an imbalance in ancestors' structure. During the session, we were able to place my mother behind my left shoulder, my father behind my right shoulder, and his father and his mother as well as their parents behind my mother (see the graphs at the end of chapter 5). The structure of this configuration allows the energy to flow so that each future generation will feel supported and loved by the previous generation, so the life force, love, and wisdom will flow from the past to the future, not the other way around. People who participate in the group process stand as representative during the process of a mother figure or father figure or any other family member. All have a chance to represent someone, based on the impulse or resonance they experience or maybe a similar life situation they had. It's like magic. Once this reparative process is done, the love flow is restored. People free themselves from the temporary roles they have taken on and are back to themselves, enriched by the others' stories of experiences and by witnessing the transformation of the person who is the main constellation character who presented a certain issue.

When we are participating in the Family Constellation, we are healing as a tribe by helping each other, listening to the stories, or witnessing the enactment of it. I was in awe again and again when people shared that some of the elements of my story affected them emotionally and that they were able to heal themselves. Synchronistically, they were brought to that particular day for the constellation process. The people who come to a session are never an accident. It magically creates a circle of trust and transformation wherein all parts are bright together and synthesized as whole. Each part of the person's situation is listened to and honored and given its own place in the ancestry tree and your own psyche.

People have great insights and healing stories after the constellations are done and share that communal healing and elevated energy of compassion and love with even initially strangers in the group, and they experience increased closeness after. Magic. Participants report healing as well as improvements in their relationships, forgiveness, and compassion, especially if there was an estrangement with family members. If individuals had an unconscious vow to the previous generations or to forgotten family members and they themselves did not have a happy marriage or a loving relationship in honor of them, now they are able to re-member (put their family members into the ancestor system correctly), find their own joy and freedom, and build a happy marriage and relationships in their own lives.

While releasing blockages and generational burdens, you may restore the loving energy flow of life from your ancestors and your parents to you. So you can connect to them through love, not through pain (as most of us do), developing strength and wisdom to deal with life's challenges and fulfill your mission, your heart's desires, and your life as an individual with your full potential.

Active Imagination to Soothe the Newborn

The other powerful moment was in healing my birth trauma, when I was able to soothe my newborn self during the Active Imagination and visualization process. I was able to see myself as a newborn baby being taken away from my mom in a birth house (a regular practice then), brought to her only to be fed a few times a day, and then taken away again and kept with other newborn babies in separate rooms till the next nursing time for the first few days after labor, till they discharged both mother and baby. That newborn baby was scared and fearful to be removed from the life-giving source and food, the mother, and away from everything she could be for the newborn child. We now know it creates deprivation and trauma when a child is separated from its mother at birth.

During the visualization process, I gently looked at the newborn baby girl and softly whispered, "You are safe. You are loved. Everything is going to be OK." I saw how "baby me" started to feel less tense and calmer. She looked back into my eyes, and I gently, lovingly touched her head and continued, "You will see your mom soon; you will survive. You will be fed." The baby calmed down even more, and I saw how she started to slowly fall asleep. Seeing the smile on her face was a delightful moment.

After that healing session, my cravings for drinking milk disappeared. I found an NAET practitioner, who helped me process and recode my trauma from the accident. As a result, the allergy slowly faded away as that fear faded from my whole being. I felt much stronger and more grounded.

Many of my clients bring up trust issues, or sometimes they report unexplainable, visceral fear of being left without resources or abandonment issues. These are some of the implications of postbirth practices. If appropriate, we carry out this visualization of soothing the newborn baby during the session. I see amazing results from these techniques.

Rebirthing with Birth into Being Practices

Almost twelve months after the car accident, I went to a workshop called Birth into Being, which was created by Elena Tonetti-Vladimirova, who has conducted them internationally for decades, helping many people by working with birth trauma, and has trained lots of professionals working with this method.

For those two days, we worked on rebirthing, "giving birth" to ourselves on a conscious and unconscious level. You go through a transformational process through module one for two days, and the last and best piece of this process is being welcomed by the facilitators as if you are the most precious person in the world at the end of the rebirthing process.

When I was slowly coming back from my inner journey accompanied by an impactful music, I heard a sweet whisper: "Welcome, dearest daughter. We were waiting for you! Thank you for coming to us, to our family. We welcome you and love you the most." My tears would not stop streaming down my face. I wiped them again and again. Hearing these sweet words in the most suggestible state reprogrammed any insecurities or negative past experiences to positive ones. The main message was "This world welcomes you, and it is for you to achieve the best, to be loved, and to be able to do anything you may think of."

I opened my eyes, and the first thing I saw through the window was the statue of a white angel that was outside in the grass behind the yoga studio where the workshop was conducted. It was the sweetest and most beautiful moment of my life in healing the birth trauma, another layer that was triggered by a car accident. I still keep the picture of an angel who welcomed me back to this world.

The next morning, I flew to Hawaii to celebrate the culmination of my healing journey. It was a rewarding time to finish the year of rebirthing myself from deep within by connecting with nature and exploring beautiful, lush gardens; volcanoes; and the magnificent ocean. It became an amazing healing journey that took me almost a year to heal from that crisis, after which I was able to come out more resilient, with more powerful resources and a stronger foundation for participating in life fully and joyfully.

The wisdom that comes from my personal experience allows me to be more present during others' journeys and to help others heal their wounds and collect their pearls of wisdom, their learnings. The lessons from life difficulties are so precious!

Would you agree that we grow the most during these challenging times? Just remember: it's not defining you but helping you to find, refine, and redefine yourself, connecting you to your inner healer, wisdom, and ancestors. You too can heal and retrieve your pearls of wisdom and transform your life!

Transformational Practices

Technique

Explore this amazing fact of your birth. Reflect and journal on this significant moment of your life. You may choose to ask your parents about your birth conditions and how you were born. Was it easy for your mother? How long did it take? Were there any complications that may affect you today? Did you have a twin?

I notice that when people work through their birth conditions and share their stories about their births, something shifts in them that makes them more complete, whole, and present, as if they have fully arrived.

My Insights

What did I learn from the story and this exercise? What are my lessons, my pearls of wisdom, I will collect here?

_____

_____

_____

_____

_____

_____

_____

What were my aha moments?

_____

_____

_____

_____

_____

_____

_____

_____

_____

_____

_____

_____

_____

_____

The cry we hear from deep in our hearts,
comes from the wounded child within.
Healing this inner child's pain is the key
to transforming the anger, sadness and fear.
—Thich Nhat Hanh

Chapter 4

YOUR PRECIOUS PART: RESTORING THE JOY AND HAPPINESS OF YOUR INNER CHILD

When the previous conditions of birth and main significant relationship difficulties are addressed, there is a possibility to work on your other significant part to reintegrate and revitalize your Inner Child. It may be done through using visualization or the Active Imagination technique (a Jungian term) to restore the joy, creativity, self-assurance, confidence, excitement, spontaneity, enthusiasm, and spirit of adventure we once had when we were children.

In psychology, we know that if children grow up in less-than-loving conditions and environments or, worse: abusive families, then they hide away their innermost selves, using this protective mechanism. Growing up as adults, they tend to become less expressive, less trusting, and more analytical. They may become locked in the past, still feeling hurt and pain. A negative past life or childhood events can cloud the present, not allowing you to achieve your full potential or become a self-actualized person.

The visualization technique I work with an Inner Child usually starts with gentle observation through a glass window or a clear door. If a person has never attended to the Inner Child, it may take time to gain trust and build a relationship with the Inner Child.

For example, for one of my clients, it took a few sessions only to establish contact with his Inner Child. The adult client had so much anger and resentment built up against his father that the Inner Child was ignoring him, until he was persistent and patient with his Inner Child to build this trust and connection.

First, he only saw the "picture" of the Inner Child, not even the child itself. Later on, he was able to see the child, who was sitting on a bench and did not notice his presence. Then, gradually, he talked to him, and later, the child was trusting enough to allow him to play with him.

The client was able to have the transformative experience: while he saw in a long-forgotten, dusty, faded image on a paper picture at first, later, he had to learn how to nurture this most important and profound relationship with his younger self. He'd ignored that part of himself for most of his life, as his father had ignored him in real life during his childhood. We often treat ourselves the way we were treated in childhood by our parents or other caretakers. We also internalize their voices, even if we may not be aware of it.

During a few sessions, the client shifted his anger toward forgiveness and released the resentment he had toward his father. Even though his father had died a long time ago, he was still holding on to that hatred and resentment, and it was affecting his relationship with his son now.

Initially, when he saw his Inner Child in the picture in his mind during the exercise, he had no awareness of this deep-seated resentment, but gradually, he gained an insight. With so much patience and accepting vulnerability, he let go of resentment. He created space for a gentle and loving relationship with himself.

He was much happier and more joyful, which resulted in his participating in singing events at the assisted living facility where he lived at that time, and he translated this to the relationship with his son, who also had anger issues toward him as well. He was able to relate to his son more genuinely and with ease, rather than with rigidity and unforgiveness. He had been angry when his son would not visit him at this facility. He was able to turn this around. It's never too late to work on your Inner Child.

The other client achieved success in a different way. She would revisit her Inner Child over and over again but at different ages, and she healed deeper layers of her wound at a different age she initially was stuck at and struggled with.

She learned how to "reparent" herself and nurture her inner self with love and care, after which she was ready to quit her long-lasting relationship with smoking. She claimed that a "poisonous partner" had always been there for her (even if it did not serve her health) since she was a teenager. She felt much stronger and more resilient to deal with cravings and withdrawal symptoms, emotionality, and vulnerability, whereas before, it would have been an impossible task. She replaced this long-term relationship with more powerful resources and a strong sense of self and self-love. She continued to revisit her younger self on her own with the app called Calm, which offers the meditation to revisit Inner Child at different ages.

She became happier and more independent and had a stronger connection to her life and a healthier relationship with food. She started to form real relationships instead of poisonous ones. Thus, her depressed state lifted to the point of joy and happiness with artistic, creative pursuits.

We have substitutions one way or another, whether with food, which was "always there"; smoking; or other addictive habits. We would rather substitute than feel hurt or experience pain from being let down by other human beings. It is safer to keep our world small. Yet once we go through the transformation and gain more resources, we become stronger and more resilient to be able to explore the world around us and keep the boundaries healthy and strong, giving ourselves nurturing and supportive words that are uplifting and expanding rather than diminishing ourselves with negative self-talk and destructive behavior. The stronger the relationship with our Inner Child, the more we experience congruency between our conscious and subconscious minds. As a result, we have much stronger resilience and more well-being in our lives.

During sessions I teach my clients how to reparent themselves, become a good enough mother, and nurture the inner self, so they can live life fully, joyously, creatively, and happily.

When I ask my clients, "How do you treat yourself in everyday life, especially in times of stress or when you make a mistake? Do you treat yourself with love, kindness, and support, or do you scold yourself for every small mistake you make?" most of the time, I find that people speak to themselves with harsh voices and words, internalizing the diminishing voices of their parents or other caregivers. One client revealed if she'd spoken to her friend the way she talked to herself, her friend would never have spoken to her again. So learn to talk to yourself kindly and lovingly as well as to your Inner Child.

Another example is of a mother who felt resentful when she did not have time for herself because her four-year-old demanded attention all to himself. She wanted to be a great mother, but that tension created incongruency in her emotional state and between her conscious and subconscious minds. When she refocused her attention by recognizing that her Inner Child wanted to have time to play as well, she started a new practice: when she entertained her four-year-old son, she brought her Inner Child into the play. For example, when she bought ice cream for her boy, she internally asked her Inner Child which ice cream she would like. She had fun buying the ice cream for her Inner Child as well and allowing her to enjoy the freedom and carefree time while spending time with her four-year-old son. She also entertained her inner girl as well or bought herself a toy while she was choosing a toy for her son. She sang cheerfully this song to herself:

I am the light, light, light. Light of my soul!
I am beautiful! I am bountiful!
I am bliss! I am! I am!

You can find it on YouTube: "Inner Child Affirmations" by Cathryn Taylor.

After practicing this regularly, she felt more fulfilled. Her motherhood became more pleasant, and her relationship with her son became even stronger. As she shared at the end of her sessions, she became "happier, more vibrant, and more alive." Using the law of repetition, she reprogrammed herself to the happiest and most creative state for her Inner Child and developed a wonderful connection with her inner essence.

As you can see, there is much more than just one healing session needed for the Inner Child. During these sessions, you can learn more about other aspects and parts of your Inner Child as well as create more trust and a more solid relationship with yourself.

After working through basic hurt and trust issues, a lot of people enjoy creativity and freedom. They are able to anchor it deeper in the essence of their being.

As an addition to guided visualizations done by a therapist during a session or meditations on YouTube, you may choose to experiment with different expressions using creative materials, such as finger painting, clay, collages, dancing, and creative writing, just for the sake of creativity, spontaneity, and joyful expression of your creative essence, which was natural to us when we were children.

Find what most resonates with your Inner Child Affirmations, and keep working with them for twenty-one to forty days, till they become part of the new you and you function as a compassionate, loving parent or observer, rather than scolding the internalized voice of the caregiver.

You can also explore the Inner Child essence on your own by finding the most suitable meditation by surfing the internet, or look for it on the apps that are readily available for any taste and length. Or find a therapist who will guide you to your loving relationship with your Inner Child so you too can experience the freedom and creative expression of your most precious part of your Inner Child. Keep your curiosity, and explore Inner Child meditation on my website. (see how to get your gift at the end of the book)

It's amazing to see how much energy a person can gain by healing his or her Inner Child and having it as a powerful resource and integrated part of her or his being and having a healthier relationship with its essence. It can be channeled for creativity or any other goals in life.

Once people can heal their fathers' and mothers' wounds, relieve birth trauma, and nurture the Inner Child, they are able to collect their pearls of wisdom and connect to their loved ones through love, not through pain. We then can have happier families, long-lasting marriages, satisfying relationships and friendships, and a healthy community and society overall. I'm wishing you all a great and liberating healing journey!

Transformational Practices

Technique

You may download the Inner Child Meditation from my website. You may write down the most resonating Inner Child Affirmations, and find the time to celebrate your inner child essence.

My Insights

What did I learn from the story and this exercise? What are my lessons, my pearls of wisdom, I will collect here?

_____

_____

_____

_____

_____

_____

_____

_____

_____

_____

What were my aha moments?

_____

_____

_____

_____

_____

_____

_____

_____

_____

_____

_____

_____

_____

_____

_____

_____

What will I do differently next time?

_____

_____

_____

_____

_____

_____

_____

_____

_____

_____

_____

_____

_____

_____

_____

We inherit from our ancestors gifts so often taken for granted ...
Each of us contains within ... this inheritance of soul.
We are links between the ages, containing
past and present expectations,
sacred memories and future promise.
—Edward Sellner

Chapter 5

ANCESTORS: AMAZING DISCOVERIES OF OUR ANCESTRY AND ITS HEALING

To all of our grandmothers and grandfathers,
to honor life flow and our previous generations who gave us life.

Healing of Ancestors with Systemic Family Constellation

Let's continue our transformational journey in this chapter with ancestors, the ones who came before us.

I've noticed that working just with biographical material does not always relieve the difficulties or challenges in people's lives fully. Once you have addressed your father's and mother's wounds following the healing birth conditions and have nurtured your Inner Child, you are able to collect your pearls of wisdom and connect to your loved ones on a deeper and more profound level. You may choose to deal with ancestral patterns now. This may address the issues between generations, such as inheritance, immigration to a different country done by our grandparents to escape difficult poverty conditions, and many others that may somehow affect the next generations. Most of the time, it is out of our conscious awareness and can be brought to light for us to see and have forgiveness and healing.

The stories included in this chapter are to honor and acknowledge our ancestors and heal dysfunctional patterns, wounds, or their untold stories that affect future generations.

Once a wound is seen, heard, and healed, then the person can move on with his or her life and stop recreating painful patterns that can be transferred from the previous generation to the next one.

There are traditions to honor and remember our ancestors and previous generations observed in many cultures. You may have heard of many rituals and days dedicated to celebrate them. For example, Día de los Muertos, in Mexico and South America, is a celebration of life remembering the previous generations who've passed. The next generation comes after, and life goes on. Those traditions and holidays are to honor loved ones and provide them with what they need on their journeys.

There are many other customs and shamanic rituals throughout the world that honor the lives that existed previously before new generations. In one of the tribal cultures, indigenous people would crush the burned powder of bones and add the powder to their food, thus keeping their ancestors "alive" in them and re-membering them their own way.

One amazing tradition came from African shamans who taught Bert Hellinger, a German psychotherapist, how to restore the flow and energy of love from previous generations to future ones and also get the blessings to live an unobstructed, magnificent life and do better than previous generations. It is done through a group psychodrama type of exercise, wherein people participate and help others to attune to the family structure and restore the proper flow between generations.

Bert Hellinger brought this to Western society and called it the Family Constellation, or Systemic Constellations. This healing modality was previously mentioned in chapter 3, where I shared how I was able to resolve complications about my birth conditions and my mother's fears that affected me during her pregnancy and labor.

During many Family Constellation sessions I participated in, I witnessed a lot of great stories, and I observed people's breakthroughs after they had been stuck in their lives. Some issues I saw included repeating the dysfunctional patterns of the previous generation, such as being unable to get married for some reason or having financial difficulties, by being loyal to either mother or father or other family members or ancestors who had been forgotten. Once the energy restoration occurred, the people were able to move on with their lives and live with much more freedom, rather than fate.

During such constellations, one person was working on a financial issue: he couldn't keep money and was always finding a way to "get rid of it." He shared that his great-grandfather had been robbed, taken away, and killed. All the properties were seized, and thus, unconsciously, the person was carrying the message that it was unsafe to have money and wealth, so he would find a way to get rid of it by investing in a wrong deal or lending it to a person who would not pay it back. On an unconscious level, the person felt he could not be rich and have what he wanted in his life because his previous generations had suffered. So did he.

While we worked during his constellation session, recreating and acknowledging this story, bringing this to a conscious level, something changed in its essence and during the group process as well. Energy shifted, and other members who participated in the process were able to release their difficulties by just participating in this process. They felt much more at ease and liberated. When people were sharing their experiences about this group process, they shared that some of them had had similar or related issues to money.

Some members resonated with having difficulties in their marriages or relationships one way or another, and some had financial issues. Overall, everybody was able to participate in both processes, and no one was left indifferent. Everybody got some healing, even if he or she was not the main storyteller participant, even if they represented part of an issue or characters in others' life stories.

At the end of the group session, during the sharing process, we created a circle that felt like one entity united by witnessing the amazing transformation of all people, feeling and empathizing with others' stories yet feeling our own individual uniqueness. Each one of us felt a different thread in a tapestry of life, being seen, being loved, and experiencing the grace and gratitude to be able to heal and learn from each other.

We listened to the song "Amazing Grace" by Il Divo, which the facilitator put on, while sharing the healing energy and closing the magnificent evening. Some people shed tears, feeling that amazing grace, and expressed love and gratitude to the group for their support and healing opportunity. What a gift to be part of that supportive human tribe!

Shamanic Healing of the Ancestors

There are many historical encounters and evidence that our ancestors had regular practices to honor and remember their ancestors one way or another, especially in tribal cultures that used shamanic journeys to connect with them.

Michael Harner and his shamanic foundation brought shamanic practices from Latin American culture. During the workshops, shamans teach how to journey and how to use the macrocosm of the shamans: connect to the upper world, the lower world, and ancestors by utilizing trance created by drumming, again in a group process, followed by sharing experiences.

During one of those weekend retreats, I chose a journey where I went to connect with my grandmother. She'd died a year prior to this experience. In our shamanic journey, we were visiting one of our ancestors, learning from the person or getting closure if necessary. For me, the reason to revisit my grandmother was to get resolution because I had not been able to be at my grandmother's funeral. I was looking for some peace and closure.

With a few drumbeats, we started our journey. I was going through a tunnel and got to the plane where my grandmother was. I met her at a beautiful meadow, where she was dancing happily. When she noticed my presence, she moved toward me with open arms and a big smile. She passed by a picnic table full of flowers and food, as if she were expecting me already and were welcoming me.

She looked very young. When she died, she was almost eighty-five. During my shamanic journey, she looked like she was in her forties, not an old gray-haired grandma who was tired of earthly life and ready to depart. She was full of life and life-force energy in that eternal plane of existence.

It seemed as if the time in this realm had stopped. She had no wrinkles and not a single gray hair. Her beautiful, sparkly blue eyes and happy smile were welcoming me to join her at the table. It was as if she were in a timeless reality where time had no impact on her. She was in a white dress that was loose and flowy. Her hair was floating in the air. She expressed absolute freedom and happiness. She looked like she was in her full power and potential and was healthy, free, and happy.

She offered me aromatic tea and some berries. We had been warned by our shamanic practitioner, "When you go to visit your ancestors in the world of deceased ones, never eat or drink anything." That was the first and most important condition for us to have this shamanic journey. Thus, I politely declined her invitation. She nodded and said, "I know. I'm not going to insist. I am glad to see you, my dear granddaughter."

She was happy to see me and expressed no sorrow, grief, or sadness. I was delighted to reunite with her as well. Since we had no restrictions on hugs and smiles, we enjoyed each other very much. We had a heartfelt conversation for some time. She asked me how I was doing. I shared with her my aspirations, dreams, goals, and life adventures.

Before my departure, the last phrase she said was "Never fear anything in life, my child."

It was so deeply reassuring that it sounded like the great phrase we hear from Buddha or Indian goddesses: "Fear not." The phrase is encoded in the hand positions of those ancient statues: one hand with the palm facing forward and up and the other with the fingers facing downward. This message gives us a hint that once we discover our true nature, there is nothing to fear.

The message from my grandmother touched me deeply, but I did not know what I would have to experience years later. It was as if she knew the secret of health and happiness in eternal life: no worries and no ill feelings, just joy, love, happiness, and peace.

I felt her loving presence as I had when I was a child with her. I was "drinking up" and "filling myself up" with unconditional love and care streaming from her essence. We were sitting during a golden sunset that seemingly never ended there. It was an eternal golden hour like you may observe at the shore of the Pacific Ocean at sunset, with golden and pink clouds in the sky—a magnificent representation of unconditional love and divine connection to loved ones and our ancestors. I wanted to prolong my time with her and continue to be surrounded by this wonderful, bountiful, warm golden energy. Loving connection to our loved ones is all we want, isn't it? That was a time of heartfelt reunion, love, and acceptance.

Suddenly, I became aware of the drumming beat increased by a shaman: she was "calling us back" to the ordinary state of consciousness. It was like in a dream: the reality started to disappear. I gave my last hug to my grandmother, turned around, and started to go back to my ordinary reality, where she was no longer in her physical form but was always present in my memories.

I felt closure and peace, and on top of that, I felt unconditional love and reassurance that she was at peace as well and that I could go back to my life reassured. As she said in one of my dreams with her before she died, "You have so much to do in this world. Go back, my dear child."

I went back from my journey the same way I had come to see my deceased grandmother. When my turn came in the circle to share the essence of my journey, I had tears of joy and gratitude. I was able to share these feelings about how we humans have methodologies to be able to change our ordinary state of consciousness and connect to a different realm to find peace, healing, and closure if needed.

In coming back from the journey, I felt empowered and renewed.

While connecting with our ancestors one way or another with different modalities, we get healing, closure, connection, and reassurance of love. We get to heal our wounds.

Below, I've included a useful exercise to connect with your ancestors. You may benefit from starting to remember your family members by naming them and researching who they were and what their life experiences were.

The first step is to name them and to know the stories about their lives and maybe to write them down and honor them by sharing the stories and restoring their presence in our lives.

Create a table for your ancestors' tree (see the example below). Make one circle for yourself, two for your parents, four for your grandparents, and so on. Fill out the names of your ancestors. Find out the talents they had and their life challenges or successes, and see where you are connected to them or different. Maybe you'll find some connections with your talents or similar patterns that run your life.

If you have an altar, you may choose to keep this table at your altar, where you can see it. If you have your grandparents' pictures on the walls, you may place it next to them. Later on, you can add more refined details to the table. Ask your relatives who are alive to know more about your grandmothers and grandfathers through stories of their lives, so you can feel more connected to your ancestors and more supported. In this way, more life force comes to our lives.

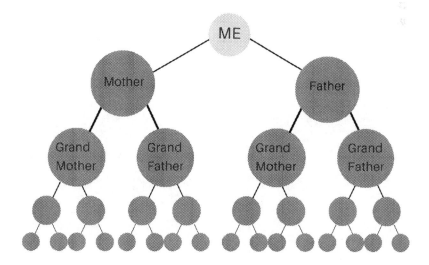

Transformational Practices

Technique

Honor your ancestors in the most honorable and culturally appropriate way for you and your family.

Collect stories about your ancestors, and create an album as a legacy for next generations, or you may explore Family Constellation healing modality by Bert Hellinger.

My Insights

What did I learn from the story? What resonates with me? What are my lessons, my pearls of wisdom, I will collect here?

_____

_____

_____

_____

_____

_____

_____

_____

What were my aha moments?

_____

_____

_____

_____

_____

_____

_____

_____

_____

_____

_____

_____

_____

_____

_____

_____

_____

What's the most important thing I learned from exploring my ancestors?

_____

_____

_____

_____

_____

_____

_____

_____

_____

_____

_____

_____

_____

_____

Part 2

FIND, REFINE, AND REDEFINE YOURSELF, AND CHOOSE A NEW YOU

This is dedicated to all my clients I have had
the opportunity to work with.
I've been able to witness your growth, your
tears, and your greatest successes.
It is my honor to guide you through those sacred journeys
now that you have chosen to have the courage to walk this path!
Much love and many blessings to all of you.

The second part offers you the chance to explore yourself as an individual with your own uniqueness through your process of thinking, your strategies, your decision-making process, your talents, things you like to do, and goals you want to achieve. Witness the stories included here, explore yourself while reading them, do your practices and journaling, cherish the work, and know that it is part of the individuation process to know yourself and how you are different from everyone else.

When you know who you are, what makes you you, and what makes you part of your family of origin, it brings the depth and courage to see the differences, so you can embrace and tolerate both the differences and the sameness. Here you will learn about the power of your mind, techniques that help to manage emotional states, and self-regulation.

First, you will learn how to find yourself and your unique personality and then refine yourself through fine-tuning of your thought process, visualization, healthier rituals, and powerful anchors.

You will learn how to choose yourself and learn about your deeper subconscious mind resources to create magical, positive changes in your life by evoking resourceful states, practicing how to make new choices, and choosing the new you every moment in life.

This part continues to take you deeper into your transformational, heroic journey. It's a continuation of the cleaning, refining process of yourself and obtaining powerful resources like those of heroes in the movies, such as Harry Potter's magic wand or the Ring of Power in the Lord of the Rings series.

But to obtain the powers, you, the hero, need to descend and do the internal work in order later to live your powers, be the hero of your life, follow your unique journey, and celebrate you. Learn about the "cartography" of the deeper part of you, and coming out from it, bring the treasures and trophies, your pearls of wisdom—new strategies, new thinking, new beliefs, new goals, and new resources—as triumphs as symbols of transformation, celebrating the new you with your friends, family, and loved ones and, ultimately, celebrating life!

The privilege of a lifetime is to become who you truly are.

—C. G. Jung

Chapter 6

YOU: FIND YOURSELF

This chapter is about you. Who are you?

In previous chapters, you have read stories about family, birth, the joy of finding the Inner Child, and connection to our ancestors. Now it's time to find yourself through your breath and heartbeat observation and create the awareness of the mind-body connection on a basic level. As well, you will find guidance for making lists of your talents and journaling. Then, in the next chapters, you will be able to learn how to master your mindset and your thought process through refining them.

In this chapter, I'll share with you simple yet powerful techniques you can use on your own to self-regulate your emotional and mental states. I use these techniques all the time with my clients and for myself as well. This will allow you to find yourself, your unique heartbeat, and your unique breath pattern. The first thing is connecting to your body, your physical essence. I'll share exercises on how to regulate your body, such as breathing and listening to your heartbeat.

Let's learn how you can "find" yourself when you feel lost or overwhelmed emotionally. In other words, how can you find yourself in the midst of the storm of life? All of us are going through the "storm" one way or another, transiting through hard periods at some point in our lives.

Minimeditation to Find Yourself through Your Heartbeat

First, find the pulse on your wrist, or place your palm on your heart, and pause. Just listen. Connect with yourself through the heartbeat. Continue this for a few minutes, and realize that it is you—your individual pattern of heartbeat, your younique consciousness. Calm awareness creates stillness in your mind. When you are aware of the beat of your heart and focus just on this process, it is easier to recognize this rhythm. This is basic awareness and observation that takes us to the first experience as babies by feeling the rhythm of the mother's heartbeat in her womb. When we connect with our heart, mindfully observing its beat, it takes us to that calm, safe, and secure place. It shifts our emotional and mental states.

Did you know that no other person has exactly the same heartbeat or cardiogram as you? It is unique to only you! As Dr. Milton H. Erickson said, "You are as unique as your fingerprint." Thus, recognize yourself as a unique expression of life, a unique human being. No one like you existed before, and no one will be like you after.

Once you connect with yourself through the heartbeat and recognize your uniqueness, with this practice, you can cultivate the expression of self-love and self-compassion. It is one of many mindful techniques. You may practice this exercise every day for a couple of minutes a few times a day, and then journal on what has changed in you. What magic appears in your life? What awareness stirs up from this observation? You may jot down your observations about this in your own journal or at the end of the chapter, where you have space for it.

With more practice in connecting to your heartbeat, you may include the observation of your breath. You may choose one or the other.

Minimeditation for Breath Observation

Start paying attention to your breath. Is it fast? Is it slow? Is it deep or shallow? Again, stop, listen, and feel your breath like the waves of the ocean; breathe in and out. Cherish yourself. Learn how to give yourself approval, acceptance, and self-love. Breathe in love for yourself, and breathe out love for others. Breathe in and out. Feel the constant movement of life force moving through you, constantly creating you. Observe this creation process in stillness for two to three minutes, and then get back to your daily tasks renewed and refreshed. Start small, with just a few minutes a day, and then you may incorporate this in your daily routine three times a day. Gradually increase to five to ten minutes. It is more beneficial to do it every day for less time rather than forty-five minutes once a week. Practicing every day, you will practice conditioning your mind, taking healthy breaks and time for yourself.

Have you ever noticed that thoughts and breath are interrelated? The faster the thoughts race through your mind, the faster and shallower our breath becomes and vice versa. Breathing deeper and slower has a calming effect on the nervous system. In addition to this, you may clear your head of thoughts and practice observing the thoughts as clouds in a clear blue sky, just watching them and not being attached to any of them. Creating this detachment helps you to observe challenges of your life from a higher perspective. Also, remember that there is always a rainbow after the storm, and the sun is always shining behind the clouds. It's up to you to change your perspective or not. It is your choice, and it's in your power.

By doing so, create space in your mind and life for something you want to focus on, manifest, and bring on. Remember, the more you focus on something, the more it shows up in your life. Have you experienced that before?

Emptying the Buffer and Filling It Up with Lists: Gratitude List, What Makes Me Feel Good, What My Talents Are

As part of the next step of continuing to "find yourself," I would like to share with you another effective technique: a journaling exercise that can also be used to release negative emotions and discharge your energy. Writing with your hand, rather than typing on the phone or computer, has more effect because when you do your handwriting, you are connected to your body. By writing out the emotionally charged state, you externalize the problem, and you have an opportunity to look at it in a more detached manner, understanding that you can change it, so it no longer defines you; it refines you.

A word of caution: make sure you have a safe space, and be gentle with yourself by scheduling a special time with this process of journaling so you do not have to rush to work or perform in life. Schedule some free time to contemplate the changes, transformation, and freedom after writing things out on the paper, so you have enough time to integrate changes and insights into your life.

After emptying the buffer, you create space for something you want, rather than negative emotions. Fill this space with what you want to manifest in your life, or create a list of gratitude: what you are grateful for today. You can start with even just one, two, or three items on the list and slowly build it up to ten. A gratitude list helps to shift your focus from what you do not have to the things you have and are grateful for. Many people practiced it, including me. It works charmingly well. Just make sure you do it consistently, and you will get the results you are looking for.

Here is the four-step process proven to be effective for my clients:

1. Journal until you empty your buffer of negative emotions or thoughts, or write about an emotionally charged situation.
2. After space is created, describe the lessons you learned.
3. After you jot down your lessons (your pearls of wisdom), start creating the list of gratitude. I call it filling up your internal space with what you want instead of negativity you discharged.
4. To conclude this practice, thank yourself for this internal work, and celebrate you.

Below is the story of how one of my clients used some of these techniques while going through her breakthrough transformational program.

Carrie listed her goals and started to journal every evening. Along with the gratitude list, she listed "My Talents" and "What Makes Me Feel Good" items so she could have a go-to when she found herself stressed while performing at her job. She reread her list of goals twice a day—thirty minutes before going to sleep and right after waking up—to set her mindset in the right direction with what she wanted and not with what the media or TV news was streaming. As a result, she was more in control of what she wanted to stream to her mind and made progress rapidly.

Find yourself through the things you like to do, what you are grateful for, what your goals are, and what makes you, aside from your family, a unique individual.

See yourself as one who has never been before and never will be again—a unique combination of genes and ancestry, character, and personality. Value who you really are, and know yourself. Dive deeper into your subconscious mind to create magic in your life. As part of the Jungian individuation process, we need to recognize who we are and how we are different from our family. The person goes on a heroic journey and comes back with a new perspective, bringing his or her tribe to a totally different way of living, as in the movie *Alpha*, wherein a young man going with his tribe for his first buffalo hunt survives the death injuries and makes his way back home to his tribe with an upgraded condition, creating a relationship with a wild wolf by saving the wolf's life because, out of compassion, he could not kill him. He was different from the others in his tribe. He was more sensitive than all the other young men.

His heroic journey takes him on a path of bringing upgraded conditions to his tribe in the form of starting to domesticate wolves and be part of human development. He needed to be different in order to bring the tribe to a different level of development; he needed to go through his painful, heroic journey to develop his strength in his uniqueness.

Each one of us goes through our own heroic journey, with a unique story to tell. Recognize your unique story, and journal it on the next page or in your journal.

Transformational Practices

Technique

In this section, you are offered to choose from a few different practices. All of them have the amazing effect of creating insight and positive changes. If you do them all one by one, you will have a much deeper map about who you are and your uniqueness. Or you may choose one. It's your call. They are as follows: find yourself through the heartbeat, witness your breath, make a gratitude list and list of what makes you feel good, and list your talents. Or you may just journal for twenty-one to forty days. Find what makes you unique and different from your family.

My Insights

What did I learn from the story and this exercise? What are my lessons, my pearls of wisdom, I will collect here?

_____

_____

_____

_____

_____

_____

_____

What were my aha moments?

_____

_____

_____

_____

_____

_____

_____

_____

_____

_____

_____

_____

_____

_____

_____

_____

What will I do differently next time?

_____

_____

_____

_____

_____

_____

_____

_____

_____

_____

_____

_____

_____

_____

_____

_____

Mindfulness is a way of befriending ourselves
and our experience.
—Jon Kabat-Zinn

What you think, you become.
What you feel, you attract.
What you imagine, you create.
—Buddha

Chapter 7

REFINE YOUR THOUGHT PROCESS AND REDEFINE YOURSELF

After you find yourself through your breath and your heartbeat by connecting to your body, recognizing your uniqueness, journaling, and listing your talents and what you are grateful for, you can now learn how to refine yourself through fine-tuning your thought process, being selective and focused, using the power of your mind, so that life challenges no longer define you but refine you.

This chapter will guide you through a few practices to refine your thought process, using reframing; focusing on what you want in life, rather than on what you do not want; mindful walking; and mindful eating.

To focus on what you want, affirmation cards are helpful. Using consistent affirmation cards and placing them on your mirror or fridge will give a continuous stream of positive, powerful messages to your subconscious mind to create the life you want, achieve your goals, and manifest desired relationships. By doing so, you utilize the law of repetition to create a positive trance rather than sliding back to the general negativity most people experience.

There are many different kinds of affirmation cards; any crystal shop usually carries them. You may buy them on Amazon, or you may google them. I use Louise Hay's cards a lot.

Another refining process is practicing mindful walking or eating, which will increase your awareness and create the magic of savoring each and every moment in your life, especially when you're eating mindfully. Eat as slowly as you can, amplifying your taste buds and enjoying the many colors and flavors, even when just eating your favorite piece of fruit. Mindful walking is to walk slowly and be aware of your body sensations, especially paying attention to your feet: muscle movement, connection to the ground, the feeling of the shoes on your feet, and so on. This will create a single focus of your attention and redirect your mind to the life process itself—to be present here and now, not to make plans for future, and not to ruminate about the past. Just be: here and now.

Try these techniques, and you will be amazed how much we may miss every day if we do not engage all our senses but overload ourselves with just visual information only, which is always readily available and streams from everywhere. Take good care of yourself, and be intentional in what you want to create in your life.

Reframing

One of the most effective techniques that will help to create change is called the Reframing Technique. It is popular in Neuro-Linguistic Programming and is also used in the breakthrough NLP coaching program. If you would like to dive deeper and learn more about NLP Breakthrough transformational program, I describe it in my chapter called "The Breakthrough with an Elevated Mindset" in the book *Master Your Mindset* in the Journey of Riches series.

So what is Reframing?

When people describe their life challenges or something they would like in their lives, they often choose a negative structure of the sentence. They use a strategy in Neuro-Linguistic Programming that is called "away strategy." Usually, this strategy gives inconsistent results because a person is trying to avoid something that brings him or her an uncomfortable or painful state. For example, poverty: "I do not want to be poor." Or health: "I do not want to be sick." Instead, the Reframing Technique redirects the mind towards what a person wants rather than does not want: "I want to be rich," or "I want to be healthy." This strategy is called towards the goal rather than away.

You can also reframe the situation by moving focus to different times or settings. For example, when parents are not happy that their children are always negotiating with them. How would you reframe it? "Maybe in the future, this skill of negotiation will serve them to become successful mediator attorneys." So the focus of your mind now has more than one perspective and releases the grip on the problem and rigidity of thinking and behavior. Then flexibility of thinking brings a different state of mind, and thus, you can make different choices in life, can you not?

Here is another example you can learn from, which Dr. Tad James, PhD, Master NLP Trainer, shared during his training about two different points of view on the same action. One client said, "My mother never loved me."

"Why?"

"Because she always set out clothes for me in the morning, and I never had a chance to choose what to wear."

Another person said, "I felt that my mother never loved me because she never set out clothes for me."

Isn't it surprising how the same interpretation ("Mother never loved me") comes from totally opposite behaviors?

Here is another example. One of my clients was irritated that her husband would always call her to ask what kind of pizza toppings she wanted for herself and the kids, even though they had been married for a decade. When she reframed the behavior of her husband and shifted from a negative point of view, "He never remembers what I like," to a resourceful state of mind, "He wants to please me by making sure I get exactly what I want; he considers it in case I want something new," that same behavior was interpreted as an act of care and love rather than neglect or ignorance. The moment she was able to shift her perspective, the dynamic in her relationship changed for the better. Isn't this interesting?

Carrie's Story: Learning and Using the Reframing Technique

Here is a great example of how reframing, a focus on what you want, and visualization were helpful during the breakthrough transformational program with Carrie, my client.

"I can't come tomorrow for the session," Carrie cried over the phone. "I injured my knee yesterday when I was running."

"I'm so sorry to hear that," I said. "Have you been helped?"

"Yes. I can walk but not run and cannot go for long distances, and it's hard to drive."

"Good. Would you consider a Zoom session instead? And you can tell me what happened," I replied.

"That will work, I guess. I'm still going to be at home."

It sounded as though Carrie were questioning if she still wanted to cancel her session: *What kind of resistance do I have? And why?* These questions were running through her head, as Carrie later shared.

We decided to schedule the Zoom session. As it started, Carrie said excitedly, "I was doing so well! I cut down my coffee in half! And I was so happy."

"How did you do that?" I exclaimed.

"I used the technique you taught me before. I listed all the benefits I would get when I cut down on coffee and substituted it with healthier drinks. I did the same for my running training, even though I would be driving back home from work. I was reminding myself about the benefits of exercise and running."

"Hey, Carrie, this is very impressive!" I said, supporting her.

"I usually run by myself. Sometimes my boyfriend will join me. He used to go to the gym while I was running, but now he feels much better around me. He even mentioned that I had changed. He noticed my eyes sparkling when I shared my vision board and bucket list with him."

"Great job, Carrie!" I said, validating her choices.

"The reframing I've learned from our sessions has worked like a charm. I even taught the technique to my boyfriend. I no longer say to myself in the morning that I *need* to run. I say I *choose* to do it and that

I'll be able to run the marathon from San Diego on the PCH toward Big Sur. Even though I know it's an ambition, I am working every day on it. But everything is gone now that I've injured my knee. My motivation is gone, and I'm off the schedule with my training sessions. My dog's condition worsened the same day as my injury, and I could not take him to the vet, so I had to ask my boyfriend to do it, causing him to have to take time from work. I felt so bad asking him to do that for me. I am such a mess!" Carrie said, crying.

"OK," I said. "Remember the rubber band? Does that take you out of spiraling down with your negative thoughts?"

"Yes."

"Good. Now, how would you reframe your current state of being overwhelmed?"

"I guess there is time to slow down and process things and reflect," Carrie said slowly, drying her tears.

"That's right! It's time to practice what you've learned about using the right mindset."

"I guess so!"

"In other words, there is an opportunity for you to make a breakthrough in your thought process and master your mindset while your body is taking a break, isn't there?"

"Right," Carrie said. "I can see it now."

"What is one step you could do today that will bring you closer to your goals?" I asked her, catching a good moment to make her focus on what she wanted and create a positive statement.

"I can continue to visualize that I'm healed and running again and can see myself participating in a marathon."

"Good! Now, when you see yourself running the marathon completely healed and healthy, do you see yourself from above or through your own eyes?"

"I see myself from above," Carrie said.

"Good! Now I want you to see yourself running the marathon through your own eyes," I said. "Feel it, and hear the sounds of people around you. Make the image colorful, and attune brightness to it, like on the screen of your iPhone. Make the sound in this movie louder, and make it more vibrant. Feel your legs running strongly and your lungs breathing in and out freely. Do you see it? Feel it? Hear it?"

"Yes!"

"Now make it even more vivid, and notice what's changed."

"I'm in the process. I am living it!" Carrie exclaimed.

"Beautiful! Practice this attunement of your sensory modalities—visual, kinesthetic, auditorial—till the next session."

At the end, we did the like-to-dislike exercise, which is popular in NLP coaching when a person for example desires to stop eating a particular food. In Carrie's case, she wanted to let go of coffee, and she did! She became free in her food choices and was no longer a victim of her old habits. She was craving changes in her life, not the coffee anymore.

At the beginning of her session, she was stuck in her limited thinking and needed a breakthrough, as the old self, old strategies and beliefs, and old mindset were not working anymore. She recognized the need for change. During this transformational process, she discovered her new approach to life, found new empowering beliefs and values, and learned self-love practices. Additionally, she began to accept help from others. She discovered a new version of herself, a new Carrie.

The complete story about Carrie you can read in "The Breakthrough with an Elevated Mindset" (see additional resources).

You learned from the previous chapter basic self-regulation and how to practice connection to your body and find yourself through the exercises of observing your breath and heartbeat and giving yourself self-love and respect as first steps. In this chapter, you have learned how to refine yourself through the thought process and power of your mind by using the Reframing Technique, mindful eating, and mindful walking. In these two chapters, you worked with emotions, thoughts, and mind-body awareness. In the next chapter, you will be invited to dive deeper into the subconscious mind that lies below your conscious awareness.

Practice these techniques on the next page, and have fun! Enjoy changing your state by reframing your point of view on the problem.

Transformational Practices

Technique

Refine your thought process: practice reframing, remember the towards/away strategy, and keep a journal about your progress. Practice mindful walking, mindful eating, and using affirmation cards.

My Insights

What did I learn from the story and this exercise? What are my lessons, my pearls of wisdom, I will collect here?

What were my aha moments?

_____

_____

_____

_____

_____

_____

_____

_____

_____

_____

_____

_____

_____

_____

_____

_____

_____

_____

What will I do differently next time?

_____

_____

_____

_____

_____

_____

_____

_____

_____

_____

_____

_____

_____

_____

_____

_____

_____

Pearls don't lie on the seashore,
If you want one, you must dive for it.
—Chinese proverb

There is no such thing as failure,
only results.
—Tony Robbins

Chapter 8

EMPOWER YOURSELF WITH HEALTHY RITUAL AND VISUALIZATION

This chapter offers you a few techniques that will help you to establish healthy rituals and connect with your subconscious mind. It's an invitation to connect to your bigger self through deeper parts of your mind and also be more in control by utilizing subconscious resources, such as the hidden magical toolbox in your life, so you can create the life you want.

Healthy Rituals as a Means to Start Creating the Life You Want

Tony Robbins once said during a presentation that he can see by looking at you what rituals you have.

I really liked it. I made a mental note about it and realized it's true. Once we have a new habit or new desired behavior, your ritual is settled. It is effortless. Hopefully, we have a healthy ritual every morning.

So what is a ritual?

It's a repeated action done with intention. Most of us in Western society have a morning ritual. What morning ritual do you have? Many of us, of course, have the morning coffee ritual. Some people have a strong morning routine, such as gym time, green juice, or a shake. Hopefully, you too can create a healthy ritual for yourself. It works like magic. You may ask why.

It uses the law of repetition, which is necessary to install new habits or new behavior. When you were a child and were learning how to brush your teeth, did your mom get flavored toothpaste or a colorful toothbrush? Did she entice you with a reward of some kind? Brushing your teeth then was an unfamiliar and new concept and behavior. As an adult, do you think about how you brush your teeth every day? Do you use your right or left hand? Most of you just do it habitually on autopilot, mindlessly, right? Once the behavior has been installed, you do not need to reward yourself for brushing your teeth anymore. It became your new norm, your habitual way of living; we brush our teeth mechanically without even thinking about it. Some of us even start up the coffee machine while brushing our teeth, right?

The law of repetition and consistency is a magic law to change your life. Did you ever see how water dripping onto stone eventually will carve its indentation into it? Be that consistent, like a dripping-water metaphor, to create refinement in your personality and your healthy habits mindfully and intentionally.

Choose something you want to change in your life, such as walking every day or anything else. Start small, so it will be easy, and gradually increase the time or distance of your walk. Make it pleasant. Perhaps listen to your favorite podcast or music, so you will enjoy it. Reward yourself for this action as well. Stick with your new habit for at least twenty-one days or, better, forty days to create a new baseline of functioning for yourself.

Diving into Your Magical Subconscious Mind

What is magic? How many of us have experienced it, especially in childhood? Is it something unexplainable? Yet we feel this, and we are in an awe state when we see it, aren't we? We all want to have magic one way or another in our lives, don't we?

Magic looks effortless. A good example is when we watch a movie in which the character is facing a challenge or is in a disempowered state, and with a snap of the fingers, at the end of the movie, we see him transformed. He reaps the rewards of life, getting the most beautiful girl, money, wealth, recognition, or success. That is all portrayed in Hollywood movies, right? In fairy tales and mythology, we see the heroic journey as well. A hero wins battles; acquires special qualities; or, like Harry Potter, uses magical tools.

What if you discover this secret of a few magical tools so you can awaken the magic within yourself by reading this chapter?

What if you acquire a magical road map that will take you to the desired results much faster and with less energy expended? What if I share with you some of the techniques that will help you to find your way in hardships or challenges and ignite the magic within?

Based on my own experience with so much work done on myself and with clients, I teach many techniques that create amazing, transformative results in my clients' lives, and I'm happy to share them with you in this chapter.

Most of you likely have heard about the conscious mind and subconscious mind, which are approximately 10 percent versus 90 percent. In other words, the

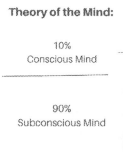

conscious mind is the goal setter, and the subconscious mind is the goal getter with 90 percent of subconscious resources. In Neuro-Linguistic Programming, one of the presuppositions is that all learning happens on a subconscious level, beyond conscious awareness.

Dr. Milton H. Erickson, a psychiatrist and hypnotherapist, was creating amazing results and positive changes in his clients seemingly effortlessly, magically. How? Through metaphors that bypass the critical conscious mind. He was very successful at that. Dr. Richard Bandler and Dr. John Grinder, the founders of Neuro-Linguistic Programming, studied his style of work and discovered the language patterns that work well on an subconscious level.

They included Milton H. Erickson's method as part of the NLP system: his style of communication directly to the subconscious mind rather than the conscious mind through stories and symbols, as in our dreams or fairy tales.

Since early tribal times, humans have learned through storytelling, when wisdom is passed from one generation to another. It's ingrained in us. We are mesmerized by movies, fairy tales, and myths that portray the heroic journey. We all like to watch the transformation and victory over challenges. You too can be your own hero of your daily life by controlling the thoughts of your mind and celebrate your victories of magical transformation. That's why you are learning these transformational techniques through the stories here in this book, isn't it?

Creating Changes in Your Life with Communication with Conscious Mind

One way to create magic is through communication with your subconscious mind. Talk to yourself lovingly and respectfully, and your body will start changing, as will your relationships and life in general. Visualization is also connected to your subconscious mind because you use images, which are the language for your subconscious mind. Magic happens especially when you utilize connection by creating congruency between the conscious mind and subconscious mind. This can be done through visualization. It's exciting, isn't it?

Based on my experience with clients, I see that one of the main ingredients is a right mindset, or elevated mindset, as I called it in my previous work in collaboration with John Spender's series of Journey of Riches books, called *Master Your Mindset*, in the chapter "The Breakthrough with an Elevated Mindset," recently published in February 2023.

Magic can be created by a professional hypnotherapist who knows the laws and therapeutic inductions and the process of creating positive changes with trance states. Or it can be done by you in learning the visualization technique or using prerecorded guided meditation.

You already know the law of repetition, as with the metaphor about water constantly dripping and refining stone. This is also used in TV advertisements: if you see the same brand over and over again, you will have it suddenly pop up in your mind when you go shopping. Online systems use algorithms as well to offer you what you liked before, right?

Constant "messaging" creates a trance state. It could be positive, uplifting, and heroic or negative and disempowered. Have you ever noticed that some people in your life have a "negative trance" most of the time? They're complaining or sharing negativity only to repeat it over and over again. In NLP coaching we call it being in a disempowered state.

How do they do this? By talking to themselves in a harsh voice, not approving of themselves, or criticizing themselves for any mistake they've made. When a person sends consistent messages to his or her subconscious mind, positive or negative, this is called self-hypnosis, or trance. We all do it every day and do not even notice. Unless we pay attention to it and consciously redirect and make a new choice of thinking, we go with the unconscious flow.

How do you create a positive outcome? You have to start speaking to yourself in positive terms and creating healthy rituals every day, using empowered anchors (which you will learn in the chapter "Be Unstoppable with Your Ring Power"), using visualization, and focusing on what you want in life.

Creating Changes Utilizing Your Subconscious Mind

When clients come in for coaching or therapy, they are in their own trance—most of the time, as I said, a negative one. Otherwise, they would not be here.

As you know already, your subconscious mind speaks in images and symbols. Remember the work of Dr. Milton Erikson and his metaphors? Visualize the desired outcome, such as winning a race, running a marathon, passing your exam, or finishing a project on time. I utilize this technique for myself to visualize my books published and feel them in my hands. It works for me. Know yourself, and choose what works for you.

It is better to practice meditation or visualization early in the morning or right before going to bed, so your subconscious mind is more receptive to your messages you want to drop to the depths. You may do visualization of your goals during the day as well. The main rule is to be consistent.

There is more than just visualizing technique, but you can start practicing with it. There's more depth you can find during my online class with weekly live Q&A sessions and group training on DrOlgaZabora.com.

As most of my clients know, to create a new behavior or new ritual, new habits use the law of repetition at least for three weeks and, even longer, forty days. Usually, twenty minutes is a good amount of time for a session with yourself. It depends how much desire, motivation, and dedication you have to create changes.

A word of caution: I do not suggest visualization when you are in a negative state, because you may not notice that you're stuck ruminating on the past rather than creating new positive suggestions. Change your state first. You want to reinforce the positive state. Use the tools you have learned so far: redirect, reframe, focus on the positive, use guided meditation, and so on. And of course, do not practice visualization in the driver's seat of your car. Change to the passenger seat if you decide to practice visualization while parking; otherwise, you will create conditioning to go into a trance state the moment you sit in your driver's seat in the car. The conditioning happens out of our conscious awareness. Have you ever noticed that when we hear our first love song or smell our grandma's cookies, we magically get to that state, and memories surface in consciousness almost immediately? This is called anchoring (chapter 10).

Story of How Amy Increased Her Confidence through Consistent Visualization

Amy was shy most of the time in her life, including when around her friends and coworkers. She wanted to say the things she wanted to say, yet she would shy away from it. One of her goals was to increase her confidence.

She shared that she felt confident and outgoing when she would volunteer at the aquarium. When she shared this positive experience from her memory bank, she lit up.

She remembered how much she knew about different fish, sea creatures, and other animals. She enjoyed it so much that she would forget she could be shy. She became totally immersed in talking to other people and kids and even giving presentations, not even thinking about being shy or hesitant. That gave me an opportunity to help her to expand her experience to other areas of her life: to the work environment and then to her friends going out. She was pleasantly surprised when she discovered that physiological symptoms of anxiety and excitement are similar: increased heart rate, a jittery feeling, racing thoughts, and heightened emotions. That was what she experienced when she was about to speak up or connect with friends or at work. It is how the mind interprets the body's signals. Every time she would practice her new thought process, she would reframe and focus on excitement and on what she wanted to create in her life. We also used powerful anchors so she would be able to get into that excited, uplifted, confident state almost instantly. One of those, the Ring of Power, you can read about in chapter 10.

The main practice she used was visualization every night before going to sleep for a month or so. Amy would come back with successful stories: she was able to point out at work meetings the mistakes she found and was able to confidently fix them. She would give rewards to herself for practicing it over and over again. Then, one day, she came to the session and mentioned that she realized she was a confident person all the time. What a magical transformation! Don't we all want that? I'm wishing you to get inspired by this example and start practicing visualization techniques along with those you have learned in previous chapters.

Continue to refine yourself, utilizing techniques for your conscious and subconscious minds. This will create magic in your life.

Transformational Practices

Technique

Practice positive, loving self-talk and visualization techniques every morning and before you go to sleep, and create healthy rituals. Choose the best practice that resonates with you at this point in your life, and stick with it for at least twenty-one days or more in order to create changes. Jot down below which practice you think you may pick up and your insights about these practices. Good luck with explorations of your positive changes!

My Insights

What did I learn from the story and this exercise? What are my lessons, my pearls of wisdom, I will collect here?

_____

_____

_____

_____

_____

_____

_____

What were my aha moments?

_____

_____

_____

_____

_____

_____

_____

_____

_____

_____

_____

_____

_____

_____

_____

_____

_____

_____

_____

What will I do differently next time?

_____

_____

_____

_____

_____

_____

_____

_____

_____

_____

_____

_____

_____

_____

_____

You are a masterpiece of your own life,
make sure you paint yourself in the colors you love.
—Unknown

The power of imagination makes us infinite.
—John Muir

Chapter 9

MAGICAL MANIFESTATION WITH VISION BOARD

You have learned in previous chapters how to refine your thought process by choosing your thoughts and focusing on what you want and the power of the Visualization technique. And you are already familiar with the conscious and subconscious minds. As an addition to all you know already, you can explore an amazing technique called a Vision Board as a method of the magical manifestation of your heartfelt desires.

Vision Board practice is widely used in different settings by different practitioners, and it's proven to be successful. It utilizes your subconscious mind's resources to get you to where you want to be in life. As you may remember from the previous chapter, your subconscious mind speaks in images and symbols. In this exercise, you will identify your goal and vision. Then search for pictures on the internet or in magazines that represent your goal. If it's a house, then find a picture of a house you would like to have. If it's a desired vacation destination, find that. One of my clients cut out a picture of Yosemite National Park, where she wanted to hike one day, and after that, she took steps to obtain a permit and announced it to her friends and got a nice group of them to hike together. Another woman found pictures of where she wanted to go on her honeymoon: Greece. For her, it was unbelievable and seemingly impossible, but a year later, she got married to a guy whose roots were Greek, and they went on a honeymoon trip to Greece!

Once all your pictures are ready, you can place them on a board, or you may use different surfaces, such as a whiteboard. You can pin them with pins or use magnets or glue. It's up to you! Always choose what works for you. You may even draw what you desire. It will work as well, as in the following story with Kelly.

Manifesting the Beach House

I was passing by one group in a training session which was working on goals. I noticed Kelly. She was one of five women who gathered together and shared their stories and practiced with each other. It seems like Kelly was mesmerized by the process of drawing the beach house of her dreams.

Kelly was the only one who decided to draw; others were journaling or writing out their goals. She was precise and concrete with her image. She drew green grass next to the beach house, a turquoise ocean, and a tree with red tropical flowers. I observed her deep meditation while she moved her hand as if it were a magic wand that would create the manifestation a few months later. Her movements were rhythmic and slow, as if she were carefully choosing how to manifest the image and to put it on paper so she would feel the most happy, free, and delighted.

She "transferred" her heartfelt desire, energy, and positive emotions of excitement to the paper by moving her hand, as if she were creating congruence between her conscious and subconscious minds. She was building a bridge between them—congruence and alignment between the goal-setter mind (conscious mind) and go-getter mind (subconscious mind) so they would align their 100 percent commitment and resources to manifest her vision. So it became clear what needed to be manifested.

I was drawn to this group of women when they started to share their goals and plans of action. When Kelly shared her goal and described the beach house she desired, the women were emotionally involved in her story organically, as if she pulled them into her energy swirl like a magnet. She shared that when her previous house burned down completely, she was forced by life to reinvent herself and start her life from ground zero. Now that her mental and emotional attachments were severed and whipped out as all her belongings were eaten by the flames of unsatiated fire, the loss created so much space that she could start from anywhere she wanted. All the space was available to her as a clean slate for her new miraculous manifestation.

She dove deeply into her heartfelt desire. What did she really want to manifest in her life?

By moving her hand rhythmically and meticulously, she created a self-induced trance and dropped that positive suggestion into the 90 percent of her subconscious mind.

While observing them and interacting with the group of women, I mentioned that since Kelly drew and visualized her house and felt as if she were already living in it, she would definitely send a strong message to her mind to get it. Every woman who looked at her drawing was impressed as well as inspired by it. When the training was over, all students traveled back to their lives, implementing their learnings.

Fourteen months later, I got a call from Kelly, and she shared her exciting news and changes that had happened by then, reminiscing about the training. Kelly suddenly said, "I got it! I got my beach house! Remember, during the training, you mentioned that I would get my beach house? And it's exactly as it was drawn that day, even the same tree with the red Hawaiian flowers on it! I can't believe it! It just happened last month."

"How?" I happily questioned.

She continued. "I was renting my studio on a Hawaiian island, and as I was passing by a board in a grocery store, I saw a picture of a house that looked familiar. I got closer and saw that it was available for lease, and it was by the ocean and close to my yoga studio. I dialed the number and was able to see the house, which was available already. When I went outside to the backyard, I was in tears. It was exactly as I had drawn it fourteen months earlier. I sat down and took a deep breath. Tears of gratitude were streaming down my cheeks, and I was amazed how things can change quickly! Let me show you my beach house."

She turned on FaceTime. I saw the tree, the ocean close by, and the sand that kissed her feet every morning, as if life were pampering her with love and abundance and rewarding her when she allowed herself to fill the space with what she really wanted.

Manifestation of Relationship

Eva was looking at her closet again and again. Finally, she had an insight. Every time she opened its doors, she would see the boxes in her bedroom closet, which were full of sentimental pieces from her past relationship, as well as tax returns, lease contracts, and other papers. She'd had those boxes packed for two years, when her ex-boyfriend had moved out. She'd packed the documents, postcards, nostalgic pieces, and other stuff, which she planned to deal with next month. "Next month" turned out to be almost two years. Finally, she couldn't take it anymore and decided to go do an NLP personal breakthrough coaching program with me.

She felt that if she unpacked it, she would not be able to pack her emotions back and hide from them again. So it was safe to put it away and not to deal with it for now. Yet every morning, she would go to her closet for clothes, and she would see those boxes reminding her that something needed to be unpacked and dealt with in order to create space for her new relationship. Once she unpacked, she would have more space to enjoy her patio and invite friends over to see the great city view from her balcony.

Finally, she got enough courage to deal with the past: past emotions, past hopes that did not happen, and past dreams. She was ready to clean up and create space for new ones.

She made a plan that she would deal with one box at a time and either find a place in her apartment and in her life for things or throw them away.

She was able to identify specific goals stated in present tense and in positive sentences: "I am unpacking my six boxes in the next six weeks and processing the stuck states and emotions, thus creating space in my house and life for my new relationship with myself and inviting a new love relationship."

She thought it was specific, doable, achievable, within a reasonable time frame, and realistic—these are the components of the model SMART, which is used in coaching, especially in the NLP model of coaching.

Once the goal was set, Eva was able to come to coaching sessions for next six weeks to deal with the past and create her new self, releasing and letting go of what no longer was needed or served her. It was a slow, painful process when she started unpacking one box every week.

The more she unpacked, the freer she felt. She found it easier to see who she wanted to become by going through the breakthrough NLP transformational program and writing out the details of the best version of herself as well as a vision of her new partner.

Six weeks passed; the cluttered past life and closet were cleaned, and space was reorganized, as well as her life and internal world.

As a result, she propelled herself on a professional level and reevaluated her values about her new relationship vision. She wrote a description of her new potential partner; it was detailed and meticulous. She would read the new vision and her lifestyle with a new partner every morning and every night before going to bed, so her subconscious mind would get the message about the desired manifestation of a new relationship. The letter consisted of a few pages that included the trips and property locations that were dearest to her heart. Her desire was resonating with a new vision, and moreover, it took new space that was created by releasing old, cluttered past feelings; limited beliefs; and unrealistic expectations of her goals. She upgraded her strategies and obtained new healthier beliefs.

She was learning how to live her new best version of herself, knowing how to set up and achieve her goals in life much more easily and effortlessly, becoming graciously attractive. Men started turning their heads when she walked by, as if she had a secret inside her.

Six months later, Eva took an international trip, only to find the exact person she had been writing about, not knowing it would happen within six months, to her surprise.

Based on what I have witnessed during my practice, it takes different time to manifest things. It can be instant manifestation, or it can take more time, depending on the goal. Trust the universe that it has its own way to deliver your results and heartfelt desires.

The leap of faith became a certainty and a new reality for Eva. She called me to wish me a happy New Year and share her amazing gift for the coming year of falling in love and entering a new year and new relationship. She now knew that by her giving the universe the grace and patience to manifest her vision and goal with gratitude, it would certainly happen.

People who get familiar with this technique get really good at it and know that it works charmingly well. By utilizing their subconscious minds' resources by drawing, painting, or creating magnificent artistic collages with amazing pictures put together, they tap into unlimited creative potential.

Some people, like Wayne Dyer, print their book covers and place them in front of themselves, visualizing that the books will be published by a certain date. He was always accurate on finishing the books around that date. It worked for him 100 percent. It may work for you too.

I personally visualize how I see and hold my books in my hands, utilizing the senses of smell, touch, and vision. With a consistent message to your subconscious mind, you will get results.

In this chapter, you have learned the magic and power of your subconscious mind and how to create positive changes in your life. In the next chapter, you will learn the powerful anchor called the Ring of Power.

Transformational Practices

Technique

Have you ever experienced this magic manifestation or participated in a Vision Board workshop? Or maybe you did it yourself or with your friends. Did you notice which way works for you? Is it a drawing, a collage, or something else? You may journal about this on the next page, so you can share your memorable successes. What resonated with you in these stories? Jot down your goals and your vision. What would you like to manifest in your life? Maybe you are inspired to create your own Vision Board.

My Insights

What did I learn from the story and this exercise? What are my lessons, my pearls of wisdom, I will collect here?

_____

_____

_____

_____

_____

_____

_____

What were my aha moments?

_____

_____

_____

_____

_____

_____

_____

_____

_____

_____

_____

_____

_____

_____

_____

_____

What images would I recollect for my Vision Board?

_____

_____

_____

_____

_____

_____

_____

_____

_____

_____

_____

_____

_____

_____

_____

_____

I believe that true transformation is possible
when genuine desire, commitment, and courage are present!
Wishing you to ignite the power of your mind
so you can live a happy and fulfilled life!
—Dr. Olga Zabora, PsyD

Chapter 10

BE UNSTOPPABLE WITH YOUR RING OF POWER

So far, you have learned a lot of transformational techniques. What a journey! Congratulate yourself for this work you chose to do. Celebrate, and give yourself a reward. Yes, that's right! Reward yourself because you are a hero—the hero of your own life, who chose to step on this transformational path. Cheers to you from my heart!

In this chapter, I want to reward you with a powerful, magical technique that has worked 100 percent for all my clients and myself. It is called the Ring of Power!

Do you remember the Lord of the Rings series? Do you remember the power that comes from having that ring? Impressive, isn't it? Do you know that you too can have the powerful resource elicited from your subconscious mind and bring it into your daily life to be unstoppable? Do you want to feel that surge of energy, power, drive, confidence, and desire to live and achieve your heartfelt desires? You can have it too!

The Ring of Power is one of my favorite techniques from Neuro-Linguistic Programming. This practice is like having your own ring similar to the ring from the Lord of the Rings.

The exercise involves the concept of anchoring, which comes from behavioral psychology, wherein stimuli and responses are paired together and create a conditioned response. The roots of this exploration come from experiments of Ivan Pavlov. He noticed that dogs would salivate before he presented meat to them. So he would ring a bell right before giving them the meat. After some time, he noticed that when he rang the bell, even when not presenting meat to the dogs, the dogs would salivate. He'd created a conditioned response of salivation to the bell sound. Today in Neuro-Linguistic Programming, we call it anchoring.

There are different kinds of anchors we experience in our lives: visual, kinesthetic, olfactory, and auditory. Here are some examples. A red light is a visual anchor; we are conditioned to stop at the red light. Another example all of you know: kids always know the looks on their parents' faces when they are in trouble. Anchors can also be olfactory: the smell of cookies from your grandma's baking or the aroma of a favorite perfume. Auditorial anchor examples could be a morning alarm or maybe favorite song. Can you think of examples of your personal unique anchors?

This process happens out of our conscious awareness. The mind is powerful, isn't it? You may ask, "How can we create powerful anchors consciously?"

Let's learn how we can bring this power of the mind to help us create the lives we want and positive changes and create a new you.

The Ring of Power is to create a positive, powerful anchor or conditioned response consciously (to receive this training as a gift from my website, see the additional resources).

I usually teach it live. We choose five of six powerful states. They are specific to an individual. For some people, the states may be confident, passionate, energized, or unstoppable. When you think about them, they make you feel you're moving forward in life and make you feel motivated. Then we anchor them to the imaginary Ring of Power you imagine in front of you. Once you've anchored those powerful states in that ring, you may use them at any moment in your life.

The states are individual to each one of us; we are all unique, as are our experiences. If you would ask for five words to describe love, for example, most of the time, even in a group of twenty to thirty people, answers would rarely match. This is one of the greatest illustrations of how we think differently and how our experiences are unique.

When I observe participants during this exercise, I see how their faces and bodies beam with the energizing wave of renewed life-force energy, which runs through them like a current of electricity. Practitioners experience this transformation, feeling powerful, feeling this resourceful state. It's like watching a transformation that takes place in the hero's body in a Hollywood movie.

Participants in this training are anchoring the powerful state into every cell, into the whole being, and shining the light, beaming nothing but strength, confidence, and power. For more information, you may find feedback from students who went through training and got results from the Ring of Power on my YouTube channel: Dr. Olga Zabora, PsyD, under the title "What people say about 'The Ring of Power' technique."

I use The Ring of Power myself as well when I need to get into that powerful state. Most of my clients love this technique. It is powerful. Like Jen, who needed that powerful, magical ring!

Jen needed to increase her confidence while teaching her classes. She was feeling vulnerable. When she started presenting her material, any slight movement in the crowd, glitch in programs with slides, or paper that was not there on time would throw her off from her path, and she would start doubting herself and even her authority in the field.

We worked on her self-esteem and limiting beliefs as part of the program, as well as creating rituals utilizing the visualization technique. She was practicing her rituals and creating congruency during the parts-integration technique. Then the time came when we decided to anchor her powerful state so she could use these techniques on her own.

I explained the exercise called the Ring of Power. At the end, I asked her to imagine a circle in front of her, colored shiny emerald green, her favorite color, just like the color of the emerald ring on her middle finger. Then I instructed her to step into the imaginary Ring of Power. As she did so, her face and whole body beamed with the energizing wave of the renewed life-force energy, which ran through her like a current of electricity. She was ecstatic, energized, motivated, passionate, and powerful.

She was anchoring the powerful state into her full body, into every cell, into her being, and shining her light. Jen was filling herself with nothing but strength, confidence, and power. We anchored these states to her emerald ring, so now she had a tangible, visual representation of her new powerful mindset.

Jen used it initially all the time, starting every morning as part of her morning routine. She would empower herself throughout the whole day. Then, with a special technique, we moved this anchor to her emerald ring she loved and wore on her middle finger. She only needed to press on her emerald ring, and she would get this great, magical effect! Isn't it amazing?

And of course, she used it during her presentations and teaching all the time. She noticed people's reactions to her changing her posture and her whole physiology. Her shoulders would get straight, her spine created a nice straight line, and her confidence in her smile and the position of her hands and legs all signaled that she was confident. Her voice would project her ease and confidence; she would move with ease; and if she encountered some unexpected change or glitch in the computer program, she would reframe it, talk about it, laugh, and move on. She would create a learning opportunity rather than internalizing this failure.

Jen became a master of reframing after the NLP breakthrough transformational program. What a success and win! She called me and shared that the moment she used this magical Ring of Power, she became a different person, the person she'd always wanted to be. She simply had not had the tools and guidance to transform herself. Luckily, she found them. It's in your power to make those empowered choices and behaviors! As Tony Robbins said, "The number-one investment you can make is to invest in yourself!"

Transformational Practices

Technique

Learn the Ring of Power practice. You may get a link to this training as a gift (scan the QR Code at the end of the book).

My Insights

What did I learn from the story and this exercise? What are my lessons, my pearls of wisdom, I will collect here?

What were my aha moments?

_____

_____

_____

_____

_____

_____

_____

_____

_____

_____

_____

_____

_____

_____

_____

_____

_____

What are the six powerful states I will anchor for my Ring of Power?

_____

_____

_____

_____

_____

_____

_____

_____

_____

_____

_____

_____

_____

_____

How could you reach the pearl by only
looking at the sea?
If you seek the pearl,
be a diver.
—Rumi

Chapter 11

UNDERSTAND THE CHANGE (UNIVERSAL MODEL OF CHANGE)

Once you have acquired the powerful resources, mastered your mindset, and healed your family relationships and your relationship with yourself, ask yourself: Are you ready to dive deeper, know about the highs and lows of the transformational journey, and learn the map to this path?

This chapter will take you on the journey of Carrie, who descended into an uncomfortable state and pain and then started making her way out with new resources, new strategies, and new choices. The Universal Model of Change will explain that process. We all go through this transformational process when we hit a crisis or have to deal with changes or losses. The uncomfortable situation gives us the opportunity to update our applications or upgrade the operating system—like on our smartphones, only here in our minds—in order for us to function efficiently when going through this transformative experience.

Carrie Recognizes the Need for a Change While Dealing with Her Pain

After tying one of her last straps and having the cameras on her gliding wings checked by the assistant, Carrie started to run off the cliff. Seeing the beautiful, lush green mountains and blue water, she took off and began to glide over Rio with freedom and tears of happiness streaming down her rosy cheeks. All she saw in her mind was the emerald ring shining far beyond the horizon, reminding her that a new goal and new state were achievable, along with new strength and courage as well. "I am flying over Rio!" screamed Carrie. She knew she was living the best version of herself.

Six months earlier, Carrie had dialed the phone number, hoping that nobody would pick up and that she would not have to leave a message. But a friendly voice answered: "Dr. Zabora, speaking. How may I help you to change your life for the better today?"

Today? Is it possible to change it all? The question went through Carrie's mind, and she felt heat coming up her face. With shaking hands, she almost pressed the Off button, but something made her stay. Maybe it was her tiredness of always being shy and not acting or stepping up when she wanted to say something or express her emotions of love and gratitude.

This time, she decided it was her chance to change things for good. So she answered, "My dog is dying," and she burst into tears.

"I'm sorry to hear that; you dialed the wrong number. I am a doctor, but I think you need to get to a vet clinic," I replied.

"I know I need help," said Carrie, swallowing her tears. "I need *your* help." She slowly composed herself and continued. "I'd like to know if I can change the way I do things. I want to participate in a marathon, and I want to change my life. I can't stay at my current job. I want to connect with friends without worrying about what they will say after I express my voice and opinions. And I'd like to fly over Rio!" She stopped, as though it sounded delusional. She did not believe her goals were possible, especially after blurting everything right at the get-go. Carrie anxiously waited to hear the comforting voice and wished for hope.

"Yes. It is possible with courage and perseverance. Everything is possible with the right mindset," I replied. "Only if you are ready for the changes and take responsibility for your new life."

"I can't continue to live in this pain anymore," Carrie said.

"When can you come over to have the first meeting, set the goals for your transformational journey, and learn what it takes for you to get there?" I asked.

"Whenever the first day is available!" replied Carrie.

"I have an opening for Friday afternoon at two. And please let me know if you need a good vet to care for your dog."

"I have a good one," Carrie said. "I'm taking him to the veterinarian today. I'll be at your office on Friday at two. Thank you, Doctor."

Carrie came to the office fifteen minutes earlier than scheduled and waited anxiously for her goal-setting session. She wrote her goals down in case she forgot them or was too anxious to say them.

I noticed she looked to be in her early thirties and was slim and tall, with beautiful greenish eyes that complemented her skin color and the curly golden-red hair tied on top of her head in a ponytail. Her puffy eyes were red from crying, and her face was pale, with freckles. She was dressed in a gray sweatshirt and sports pants that hung on her loosely. She wore no jewelry, just a tiny emerald ring on her pinkie finger. The only bright elements about her were her sneakers, a charming fit. When I mentioned them, she replied that wearing good and comfortable running shoes was important because she was a runner and swimmer. I noticed she was nervously playing with a rubber band. I asked if she knew she could use it for her benefit.

Even though everything hinted that she had a stuck mindset, she was surprisingly receptive to hearing more about the technique, which was to put the rubber band on her wrist and snap it (not too hard) when she caught herself spiraling down into negative thinking. The goal was to snap herself out of the negative trance. It became the first technique she discovered that day, and it worked amazingly well.

As I learned later, Carrie had been born in Australia, and her parents had moved to the United States when she was around two years old. She was still living in her parents' house. She had two dogs; one was an eleven-and-a-half-year-old basset who had back joint issues, could not go for long walks, and needed extra care. He was on a special diet and was not eating well, so the feeding process was like taking care of a baby. Sometimes injections needed to be done. This was Carrie's favorite dog, as she had raised him since he was a puppy. They'd had many fun times together, and her anxiety was through the roof, as she knew he could die at any time. She wondered if she would be able to cope with the transition. Carrie had another dog: a female chihuahua rescue dog that was around three years old and happy like a puppy, which Carrie had gotten last year. The chihuahua gave her some comfort and brightened her days, she said.

Carrie and I talked in my office for about an hour. Then, with her guard finally down, she breathed out loudly and forcefully and said, "That's it."

I offered her chamomile tea and let her stay in that empty, full-potential state. When she was bringing her painful and stuck conditions to the table, her speech was significantly influenced by limited thinking. But by speaking up in the right environment, Carrie made the space inside that she could now fill with a new way of thinking that could propel her forward in life. She could focus on what she wanted instead of what she'd carried inside herself before.

Carrie and I started working on her goals so she could fly symbolically and literally to where she wanted to be instead of being stuck. No one's goal is big or small. It depends on the person and circumstances, as it was for Carrie. Her short-term goals were clearly defined, and she wanted to feel unstuck in her choices. She wanted to run her marathon and, thus, desired to be motivated to run every day. Her biggest dream was to feel freedom and fly over Rio de Janeiro. But to travel to Brazil seemed impossible with her old mindset and where she was currently in her life and work.

We collaborated and both worked hard. I provided her with the best result-producing techniques I knew, and she did everything that needed to be done, including the tasking, the exercising, and the practicing. We met weekly for two-hour sessions to learn about her strategies and painful, stuck states and discover how she thought and how we could change her thoughts and, most importantly, her beliefs.

Over time, I noticed Carrie was beginning to walk in a livelier and more energetic manner. The life force would start flowing through the movements of her legs, making her feel stronger and more grounded, as she said. She also chose to wear blue instead of gray now. Blue was her favorite color, the color of the blue ocean, she said. The compass of her mindset slowly began to change direction.

During one session, while we talked about her progress, I said to her, "Do you know that the name Carrie means 'free' or 'being free'?"

Her green eyes sparkled like two precious emeralds fired with passion and life force. She replied, "No! This is the first time I have heard that. How funny that I've felt the opposite most of my life. I've felt stuck at work and with my relationships, coping with the stress through so much coffee."

Carrie listed her goals, dream travel destinations, and "What Makes Me Feel Good" items so she could have a go-to when she found herself stressed while performing at her job. She reread her list of goals twice a day—thirty minutes before going to sleep and right after waking up—to set her mindset in the right direction with what she wanted and not with what the media or TV news was offering. As a result, she was more in control of what she wanted to stream to her mind.

She was able to go through her pain and make her way out to a new level of functioning by obtaining new resources through the Ring of Power, reframing, and the other transformational tools you read about earlier in this book, which we choose to learn how to use in order for us to transform ourselves.

Universal Model of Change Explanation

We all go through changes, challenges, and difficulties at some point in our lives. We all experience life transitions, including changing homes, losing a job, getting a new job, and having periods of adjustment, such as divorce, an empty nest, or grief. Not to forget that we just went through a global pandemic, lockdowns, isolation, and losses. This illustration of the Universal Model of Change is widely used and taught in advanced Neuro-Linguistic Programming trainings.

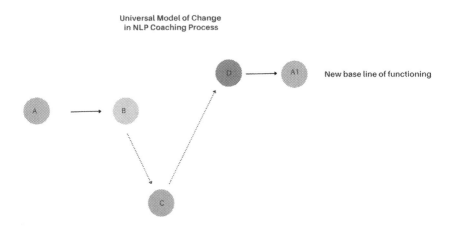

The Universal Model of Change serves as a map or a journey of transformation from A to B to C to D and, finally, to A'. The graph shows the turning points of the journey.

This Universal Model of Change shows that at point A, a person may live a normal life; nothing out of the ordinary happens. The person uses a habitual way of thinking and behavioral pattern and familiar strategies and ways of living.

Then, at point B, things change. Either the person feels stuck and becomes aware of the need for change, as you read above in the example with Carrie, or a significant emotional event happens, such as a car accident, divorce, loss of a job, or other challenge. The person no longer feels comfortable with the previous life flow.

In the Universal Model of Change, it is the descent from B to C. In the alchemical language of transformation, when we are dealing with pain called blackening, it is a descent to the depths. There is a need for change. At point C, the person hits rock bottom and is in crisis. Then the person looks for a solution because the old strategies are not working anymore. After this dive in, the hero experiences the second stage in a transformational process, called, in alchemical language, whitening, or doing the laundry, as you may remember. In the Universal Model of Change, he or she goes from point C to point D. The person may get help in the form of therapy, coaching, healing groups, or transformational retreats.

The more work is done, the more people get aligned to their new visions and new goals. On the way to point D, synchronicities start to occur, as in case with Carrie (chapter 17). The person acquires resilience and new resources and is able to deal with life changes with a new, upgraded "operating system" and "apps" to function in an optimal way.

When a person gets from point C to point D, he or she acquires more resources, new behaviors, new thinking, and, thus, new functioning. Once habituation happens during this new level of living at point D, the D eventually will become level A', which becomes the new normal, and then life continues with new resources, experience, and wisdom (pearls of wisdom)—his or her own unique pearls that he or she dove into the depths for and had courage to retrieve. That wisdom brought change as a result of this journey.

As long as we go through this process from C to D consciously and recognize that we are changing, we will be able to consciously create transformation in our lives.

Now that you have learned the Universal Model of Change, you will be able to recognize the turning points and use them as a map for your transformational journey. Journal on the next page about your experiences with the map of changes you just have learned. In the next chapter, you will explore how to live your new choices, new behavior, and new you.

Transformational Practices

Technique

Having a map for your journey, you may journal about your successes
to solve the challenges or your journey you took to transform yourself.
What are they?

My Insights

What did I learn from the story and this exercise? What are my lessons,
my pearls of wisdom, I will collect here?

_____

_____

_____

_____

_____

_____

_____

_____

_____

_____

What were my aha moments?

_____

_____

_____

_____

_____

_____

_____

_____

_____

_____

_____

_____

_____

_____

_____

_____

What will I do differently next time?

_____

_____

_____

_____

_____

_____

_____

_____

_____

_____

_____

_____

_____

_____

_____

You are never too old to chase your dreams
—Diana Nyad

Chapter 12

CHOOSING AND LIVING
YOUR NEW YOU

In this chapter, let's learn how to redefine yourself through new behavioral choices, new thoughts, and living your new you, your best version of yourself. You already learned about powerful resources of your conscious and subconscious mind. Now it's time to live your power. You might ask yourself, "How would I do this?" You know from the previous chapters how to refine yourself through your thought process, and now you will learn how to redefine yourself.

You have a vision of your goals and what you would like to achieve; now, by making new choices, thinking new thoughts, evaluating your beliefs, and being consistent in your behavior and thought process, you will create a new you. While doing this, please be patient with yourself, and yes, magic will happen. Every time you choose a new you, you are choosing a new refined and redefined version of yourself. Praise yourself, and value yourself; you are shining the light for others. Blaze your trail. Share your wisdom and learnings with others.

Remember that by making new choices, we fire new neurons, and we wire them by practicing new models of behavior and new thought processes. We literally recreate a new person who thinks like a success and acts like a successful person. Whatever was unattainable or seemed like magic now is our new daily routine and new homeostasis. Learn something new, and practice every day to live your bigger self. Make new choices and new thought processes. This means you can live your new self in a new level of consciousness with new resources. This represents a new level of functioning named A', according to the Universal Model of Change you learned in the previous chapter (see chapter 11).

Carrie Lives Her New Choices and Best Version of Herself

Carrie was emerging from her depths and was getting to the "new-normal" level A'. She acquired her new resources and was able to function more optimally and congruently to her desirable state and resources after having her breakthroughs.

After a few NLP coaching sessions of deep transformational work, Carrie showed up to a session in a beautiful silk blouse with green, blue, and turquoise colors. In an energetic, almost dancing manner, she reflected with a big smile that her sparkly inner waters were clear and calm, and her inner sky asked for its gliding. We had done the internal cleaning process, and gray clouds were disappearing from Carrie's horizon as more clarity and confidence showed up in her, which were reflected in the external events of her life.

"I went to an interview this week for a new job!" Carrie said right at the beginning of the session.

"Yes! This deserves celebration and acknowledgment. Reward yourself for each success, no matter how small or big! Your mind needs this confirmation!" I matched her in her happy and exciting voice.

"Most likely, I will get the job," Carrie said. "So I can save up some money for my trip to Brazil."

"Wonderful!"

"And I found a school where I can learn hang gliding!"

"Yes!"

"I no longer need coffee to energize myself," she added.

I'd noticed that lately, she was filling the sessions by describing her new choices and changes, rather than my pouring into her.

"When I was driving here, I had all green lights on the road. So I guess it's a good sign." Carrie continued verbalizing her thoughts.

"Yes. Absolutely! Now, are you ready for another challenge?" I asked to check how strongly planted she was in her new mindset.

"Yes!" she said.

"OK! Now you know about the synchronicities you just experienced while you were driving today to the session. Collect these occurrences in your journal for two weeks, next to your gratitude list. Then focus on what you want to use your new mindset for intentionally. Finally, let your unconscious mind know that you notice its symbolic language by keeping a record of your dreams and practicing your new behavior and new choices."

"Deal!" Carrie's beautiful smile shone.

"OK. Great. Now would you like to seal your deal with the most powerful anchoring technique that will be available to you all the time?"

"Of course!" she readily replied.

We scheduled follow-up sessions for two weeks later and then a month later, so she could have time to practice living her new choices and behaviors.

During the two-week follow-up session, Carrie shared that she was adjusting to her new job and getting to know her coworkers. She'd replied yes to a work email invitation to run for her company's half-marathon event. Before, she would never have been able to do that; she would have shied away from any challenge and gone with the flow, even if it didn't serve her or if her gut feeling and intuition knew that a hiking group could go in the wrong direction. She had now learned how to trust herself and her internal voice, be true to herself, and provide love and respect to herself. The results of this new mindset could be seen in the outside world. She was living her life with the power of the green light of the emerald ring she anchored in her mind and body.

A few months later, I got a short letter from Carrie with a small picture of her in a beautiful, bright, flowery tropical dress with shiny green and blue colors.

> My dog passed away a few weeks ago, but beforehand,
> I created an album about my best times with my dog
> and celebrated his twelfth birthday with my friends and

family. I focus now on the love I had for him, knowing that he had his own time and that I provided the best care he deserved. I'm leaving behind, with love and gratitude, what has been dear to me—my memories— and I'm keeping what I need: love, lessons, and my wisdom.

PS My boyfriend got a job in Rio, and I'm flying there to see him in a couple of weeks!

I could see in my mind how ecstatic she would be while flying over Rio.

"I am flying!" Carrie screamed out of happiness while she flew over Rio de Janeiro, knowing she was in constant creation of her life. By then, she knew that whatever she focused her mindset toward, she could achieve. She'd discovered the magical toolbox inside her mind. She saw everything from a bird's-eye view, including her past problems and challenges, as the roads in her life streamed together like the streaming rivers she saw below. The memories intertwined like the silver lining thread woven into our colorful tapestry of life, with its ups and downs, success and growth, tears of grief and tears of happiness. Carrie circled over the valley. She was free from fear and pain and enjoyed her freedom and power. She knew she was living her best version of herself! She was celebrating her new Carrie.

I know that if I believe in my clients' potential to change (and I always do), they will believe in it too, and they will have the opportunity to turn their lives around, live the lives they've always wanted, and have the courage to go through this uneasy and sometimes painful but gratifying transformative process.

You have discovered your new self, the new you! It's time to live it! Celebrate the new you!

Are you ready for more?

In the final part of this journey, part 3, you will be offered the chance to explore even deeper parts of your being: your soul story, deep meditative processes, and practices that can take you to profound discoveries in your journey to wholeness.

Transformational Practices

Technique

Write the Best Version of Yourself. You may include previous lists of what makes you feel good and what your talents and your goals are. Make it vivid and detailed. Once you are done, read it to yourself, and ask yourself, "Does it give me energy? Does it excite me? Does it motivate me to act?" Or do you need to tweak it to feel the power from your new vision of yourself? Make sure you write it in positive sentences and present tense. Once it's ready, read it a few times a day, and visualize yourself making new choices and behaviors for twenty-one or forty days, celebrating the new you!

Best Version of Myself:

My Insights

What did I learn from the story and this exercise? What are my lessons, my pearls of wisdom, I will collect here?

_____

_____

_____

_____

_____

_____

_____

_____

_____

_____

_____

_____

_____

What were my aha moments?

_____

_____

_____

_____

_____

_____

_____

_____

_____

_____

_____

_____

_____

_____

_____

_____

Part 3

DIVE DEEPER INTO YOUR SUBCONSCIOUS MIND TO FIND YOUR BLISS AND FREEDOM

This is dedicated to the divine wisdom
that resides within us that guides us
toward wholeness and healing.
When we are connected to our inner whole self,
we are creative, we are free, and we are blissful.
May you achieve your wholeness and
healing you are searching for.

The third part of our adventure allows you to find yourself in the depths of your psyche through witnessing the journeys of others. These stories of the depths and heights of the soul journey will give you the chance to retrieve your pearls even more precious than in the second part—of course, if you are ready for it. Here you have the opportunity to witness the process of expansion of consciousness, finding the bliss and freedom and then bringing it back to its ordinary state of consciousness to live it.

As you remember from the beginning about the transformational process described in the introduction, after recognizing the pain, you started your "whitening" (in alchemical language of transformation), or your inner cleaning process, by recognizing old patterns and strategies that are not working anymore; discovering new strategies; choosing a new you; learning about yourself as a separate, unique state of consciousness; reconnecting with yourself and family members on a new level; and working with family wounds and ancestral healing. So you have experienced the feeling of belonging to your tribe and then recognized your uniqueness.

Now, in this part, you will be able to continue to witness the albedo (whitening) stage while journeying through the depths of your being. You'll find stories that will take you to deeper parts of yourself beyond conscious awareness, which means to dive into your subconscious mind to retrieve your pearls from the depths of your being through stories of past-life and life-between-lives meditations, the dream realm, and transpersonal practices that guide us to the deeper part of ourselves.

Having those examples makes us chart our one trajectory in transformational journey heights and depths of the human psyche. Get those pearls, and bring them to your conscious level so you can expand your consciousness with new insights and learn how to integrate these experiences into your life.

Chapter 13 will talk about the healing power of dreams. It will help you to see how you can interact with your subconscious mind on a deeper level, even your soul's deeper callings. Chapters 14 and 15 will guide you through soul journeys with regressive hypnosis. Chapter 16 will share the blissful states of consciousness through Holotropic Breathwork™, which is accessible to us once we are willing to do the work. The last two chapters, 17 and 18, offer you methods to recognize if you are on the right path, integrate your new experiences, learn and live the insights and aha moments, bring the new you to daily life, and live your new version of yourself.

The dream is the little door in the innermost and
most secret recesses of the soul,
opening into that cosmic night which was psyche long
before there was any ego consciousness.
—C. G. Jung

Chapter 13

HEALING POWER OF DREAM

The mist was so heavy that I couldn't see through it. The visibility was so low that I had to step slowly and very carefully. I came closer to something I could barely see—undefined figures. Slowly, visibility occurred. Two huge statues of elephants emerged from the fog. They were gigantic. I saw myself walking down the path toward them. Other people were walking on that path as well. The two huge golden elephants guarded the entrance to a special place called the Land of Sacred Elephants. Their ears were full of diamonds encrusted along their earlobes. The mist started to disappear, revealing their monumental size. Finally, I was able to reach them and get closer so I could touch them. At the moment of connection, I felt a great feeling of awe, as if grace or something magical were transmitted to me and changed my essence. At that moment, I woke up.

I carried that feeling of awe throughout the whole day. I had that magical mist and almost like a flavor of the dream inside me and around me. I moved throughout the day almost like flying, gently moving through life, feeling trusting, in sync with my conscious and subconscious minds, feeling that congruency.

This is how it usually feels when your dream is interpreted the right way and hits the resonance point. It feels as if you've touched something sacred within you, and it reveals its secret and sacred part of your being. It reveals the hidden, divine part of you, something you will not be able to access otherwise. It's magnificent and magical. In Billy Joel's song called "River of Dreams," he says he is searching for something in the middle of the night: "Through the jungle of doubt / To a river so deep / I know I'm searching for something / Something so undefined / That it can only be seen / By the eyes of the blind / In the middle of the night," meaning we can only see what the soul is revealing with closed eyes, through dreams. What a beautiful, symbolic image for dreams of the psyche and its realm.

I have been collecting my dreams since I started to go through psychoanalysis at eighteen and had my introduction to this mystical realm through *The Interpretation of Dreams* by S. Freud then. The world of dreams has been fascinating for me since then. Later, I practiced lucid dreaming as well and signed up for Jungian courses to learn how to interpret the symbols of dreams. Years later, I got into the certificate program of the C. G. Jung Institute of Los Angeles, where I had an opportunity to go through dream analysis with a Jungian analyst to be able to shed the "mist" from dream symbols and "see clearly" material from my subconscious mind.

C.G. Jung
Personal Concious, Personal Unconscious,
Collective Unconscious

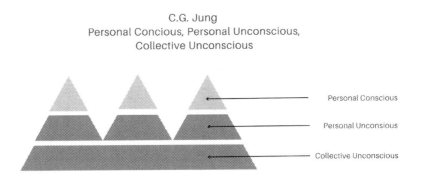

Personal Conscious

Personal Unconsious

Collective Unconscious

This graph shows the idea from C. G. Jung about how much material is available for us on a conscious level and in our Personal Unconscious. We all share the Collective Unconscious. We tap into Personal Unconscious and sometimes Collective Unconscious material through dream material. We all have individual parts, as you can see, and we have common, shared unconscious material. In that depth, we are all connected.

Messages through Dreams

When I was able to bring this unconscious material to my dream analysis, I was able to find the repeating symbols, scenarios, and people in my dreams. I also had precognitive dreams about loved ones or family members. For example, I would see my mom in my dreams if she wanted to talk to me. I would call her and ask what she wanted to talk to me about. She would be surprised—how did I know? My answer would be jokingly "Through my special sky-line phone" (my spiritual iCloud). I'm offering just a few examples below of symbols my clients bring to sessions. There is an unlimited number of symbols and variety. It's all younique. It's all about you and your journey. See what is familiar and what comes up for you while reading this chapter. Jot down your reflections in the section "Transformational Practices."

Shoes

In the dreams I witnessed from my clients and in my own, I found repetitive symbols or images, such as shoes. From time to time, different kinds of shoes would show up in the dream. People would try out new shoes. What do you think it may mean? It may signify trying out new roles in life. I've noticed that those dreams happen when people are about to move to a new path on their journey. They dream about new or different shoes and try them on.

> Miniexercise: Have you ever dreamed about buying or trying out new shoes in your dreams? If so, write them down, and notice when they occur.

Suitcases

Another interesting theme that shows up in dreams is the packing and unpacking suitcase. Sometimes people dream of losing suitcases filled with old clothes. This happens when a person needs to let go of old stuff or an old way of living.

Miniexercise: What symbolic way is your personal unconscious talking to you when you need to leave the old behind? Jot down if you remember any examples. They are precious.

Laundry

One of the great symbols I've noticed repeating is "doing laundry." Laundry is an alchemical symbol of cleaning, meaning working through your inner challenges. I was doing "internal laundry" a lot when I was in therapy during my psychology years. This metaphorical image of cleaning up your stuff was in the story with Carrie in part 2 of the book: we were cleaning her internal "clouded sky" (meaning to clarify new strategies, new beliefs, and new behaviors) so she could fly freely, symbolically, psychologically, and literally over Rio de Janeiro by gliding.

Miniexercise: What symbolic way does your personal unconscious talk to you when you need to clean and make space for something new? Did you ever have any dreams about cleaning or washing something? Was that connected to your life literally or symbolically? Jot down if you remember any examples. They are precious.

Childhood Dreams

Did you have repeated childhood dreams? Most of my clients did. I had mine as well. It was about flying over my apartment building and seeing my parents way below and flying through the dark sky into an endless sky full of stars. I had this same dream a few times during my childhood. Have you noticed that lots of people fly in their dreams?

Miniexercise: Did you have recurring childhood dreams too? If yes, jot them down at the end of the chapter.

Houses in Dreams

My clients often bring an image of a house to a session. A house is a popular symbol. It may symbolize you as a structure in the majority of the dreams. It could signify a literal house as well or a symbolic image of a house or even a deeper meaning on an archetypal level. There are different levels of interpretation: literal, symbolic, and archetypal. There is no cookie cutter for dream analysis, even though the same symbols can appear in different people's dreams. It's an art of dream interpretation, not a job.

One of my clients brought to therapy a series of dreams about repairing her house. In her dreams she always tried to repair it with her husband's involvement; it was an unconscious attempt to repair or remodel the relationship with him. Once she was divorced, she started to have a series of dreams about remodeling her house on her own. At the end of the therapy, she had a dream about finishing the remodeling of the house, and she did it herself. She suddenly had the realization that she had closure and felt complete with her ex-husband's relationship.

Another great example was a dream wherein a person was revisiting her childhood house, where the old wires were installed as new. Before that, she had in her dreams just paintings or walls that were repaired in the house. But years later, her dreams about the house shifted, and she saw the house being rewired fully. She felt she had "remodeled" and "rewired" herself from the inside out by finishing the deep work on herself after years of analysis. Her childhood house was fully "rewired," signifying that her whole personality was remodeled as well. What a communication from the Personal Unconscious!

Miniexercise: Did you see a house in your dreams too?
If yes, jot the dreams down at the end of the chapter.

Ways of Working with Dreams

It's easier to interpret a dream when you have a recollection of recent events in your daily life, and you may see the connection to symbols and events. To help this, keep a journal of your dreams, and refer to previous ones that have repeated symbols in them. The more consistently you keep track of your dreams, the more your subconscious mind will communicate with you through symbolic images of dreams. You may create a new habit of keeping the journal next to your bed, or you may dictate your dream to your phone. The images in dreams most of the time disappear like the mist in the dream of the Elephant Land I had that day. It is very useful to write down a dream right after you wake up.

When images are not clear from your dream, you may try to draw them while in a light relaxed state, allowing your subconscious mind to let it surface and come out, even if it's just one element of the dream. Afterward, you may hang it up to see them consistently. Your subconscious mind will start to reveal more information, meaning, and new insights. Some of the images can stay with you for years, like childhood dreams, and some images will disappear immediately the moment you wake up.

During shamanic seminars working with dreams, we would create a song, poem, or dance of our dream. This way, you can integrate your unconscious material deeper into you. I know that other traditions include the sharing of dreams during breakfast from the family members, thus creating an example for children to pay attention to their unconscious material and create deeper connections to themselves.

> Miniexercise: If you had any, what customs or traditions
> did your family have about sharing dreams?

When my dreams were witnessed by a Jungian analyst, it was helpful and created the conditions to see clearly and make sense of them. I could identify a theme that would be a thread for a few months, keeping the same symbol repeatedly until I got the message or solved the problem.

An indescribable feeling of being understood, when getting a message from your psyche, comes from a dream being interpreted the right way. Thus, it helps you to propel yourself into different levels of development and growth. Besides the insights you may gain from the interpretation of your dream images, you need to change your behavior to embody this new perspective in life. Treat those pearls from your subconscious mind as treasures; value them. The more you do it, the more conviction and confidence you will discover of your unique truth inside you.

Precognition Dreams

Sometimes people see dreams that may predict the future. Have you ever met anyone who shared a dream that was predicting the future? C. G. Jung was exploring deeply his Personal Unconscious and dove into the Collective Unconscious as well. He shared his experiences and symbols in his *Red Book*, which was published a long time after he died. His explorations were deep in the dreams he shared, and some of them were precognitive.

Three months before my grandmother passed away, I had a series of dreams.

The first one happened three months before she died. It was the middle of August, and I had a dream about my grandmother running away from me. I finally found her at some kind of small office building, and the lady at the front desk, once she saw both of us, pointed a finger at the clock and said, "It's Leo time." We both looked at the clock, and surprisingly, instead of numbers, there were the astrological signs, as if it were the time of the astrological sign of Leo—and yes, it was August! Once I woke up with a heavy heart, I checked on how my grandmother was doing. And true, my grandmother needed to be taken to see a doctor.

In the second dream, which happened a month before she passed away, I walked on an empty road with my grandmother alongside. She wore her favorite turquoise coat and white hat. It was getting darker. After some time, she stopped and said, "OK, my dear granddaughter, now I'm going to stay here." I immediately responded that it was unsafe and said I would not leave her in that empty, dark place. She replied with a smile while pointing to the city lights far away, "Do you see those lights? You have to go there; you have so much to do there. I'm done. I'm going to stay here."

I woke up in my attempt to hug her, and she disappeared as my dream slipped away from me. It was as if she had told me that her journey was over and that I had to stay in this realm and continue with my journey that my soul had planned for. I cried tremendously, realizing she was going to depart this life soon. This dream happened a month before she died.

The third dream was the night she died. She was in a mountain cabin made out of round logs. I saw her folding her beautiful clothes gently and slowly with love, specifically the clothes I had bought for her as a gift. Her pink blouse she liked the most; she looked beautiful in it. I asked what she was doing, and she replied, "I'm packing. I'm leaving, my dear granddaughter."

I woke up in a state of anxiety and grief. Right at that moment, I got a call from my brother, announcing that my grandmother had just passed away. I was speechless.

My dearest grandma was my safe haven, with such an easygoing, great, happy attitude in life. From her, I learned how to reframe and focus on the positive in life since my childhood. Her laughter, smile, unconditional love and care, and essence were able to live and exist on earth in the human form of my grandmother. I was in tremendous grief and loss, but at the same time, knowing that she was able to communicate with me through dreams made me be able to be strong and live through the loss and pass through the feelings of emptiness.

The wooden cabin seemed like it was a wooden coffin she was buried in three days after Thanksgiving Day, the day she died, the day when we all give thanks to our families and loved ones. That day, my thanksgiving was only praying for grace and giving thanks to the higher realms that her soul would find peace and home there as her body found its home in Mother Earth.

Forty days later, I had a dream wherein I saw myself as a teenage girl holding the hand of my seven-year-old brother, walking with him outside. We saw our grandmother far away in an alley. My grandma was walking away. I said to my brother, "Grandmother is leaving. Let's go.

Let's run and get to her." We were running and running and running endlessly, but we could not reach her. Her image slowly disappeared from the horizon.

It was as if her soul, after forty days, departed from the earth plane and said a final goodbye to me. Since that time, I see her in my dreams occasionally, as if her journey was complete and mine is not yet.

> Miniexercise: Journal about and reflect on your most impactful dream.

Honor your dreams, and honor yourself through your dream life. Create art if you feel like it, dance it through, and connect to your unseen realm. Dreams have so much wisdom. They are unique to you, to your journey called life!

Precognition Dreams about the Dog Dying

With the next story, I would like to share an example of connection not only to our human family members but also to other family members, our pets. We are connected to them as well.

A few years after the loss of my grandmother, my dog was diagnosed with cancer six months prior to his death. During that time, I saw him in my dreams three times. In one dream, I tried to save him from boiling water. I found him and was trying to keep him high above the water. It was the time when I was looking for a solution and possibility for surgery.

In the second dream, I tried to catch him in my arms while he was falling from the sky, and I missed catching him. I woke up in grief, devastated that I could not save him. This dream happened when he was put on steroids by his vet.

In the last dream, I saw him walking under heavy rain in the park, on a steep and slippery surface, like sliding on an avocado on a slippery floor. I tried to put the leash on him but unsuccessfully. Sliding on the slippery ground under the rain, I could not catch him.

Realizing he was leaving this world, I woke up in tears again.

A month later, he had to be put to sleep, on Presidents' Day. It was best for him to stop his suffering. Since the tumor was blocking his bladder, the doctor warned me he had to either die from the rupture of his bladder if I took him out of the hospital or be put to sleep. There was no choice. He fell asleep with honor and unconditional love and loyalty in his eyes.

That Presidents' Day was windy and cloudy. But the moment my dog's soul left his body, the sun's beautiful, bright light shone through the open door as a reminder of him being a sunshine light for me and all those he would greet and meet happily by just walking on the street. He was "golden" inside and outside: he was a mix of a golden retriever and chow chow. With his golden personality, he was sunshine inside, and he had golden fur on the outside. He was precious, like all of our furry family members.

A few days prior to his departure, I lay down next to him, looked him in the eyes, and said, "You did your part. You showed your unconditional love, so you do not have to suffer. I will always love you. Thank you for your love. You are my sunshine and always will be."

Stevie Wonder's song "You Are the Sunshine of My Life" coincidentally was playing on the radio station when I left him at the clinic, sleeping forever. I drove home feeling the empty abyss that can never be filled again and the endless loss, with eyes full of tears and blurred vision, feeling that part of my life had gone and part of my heart as well.

Endless rivers of tears were streaming down my face for days after his departure, like the rivers of our dreams. In Billy Joel's song "The River of Dreams," he says "we all start at streams," and "we all end up in the ocean." Our "rivers of dreams" end up in the ocean of dreams, as if our Personal Unconscious takes us to the Collective Unconscious we all share. We are all connected. We all have access to deeper wisdom through dreams. What is your experience with dreamland? Journal on the next page.

Transformational Practices

Technique

If you remember your dreams, what are your repeated symbols in the dreams? How did you grow up as a child with the custom to share or not share your dreams? Keep a journal of your dreams regularly to keep communication and build a relationship with your subconscious mind.

My Insights

What did I learn from the story and this exercise? What are my lessons, my pearls of wisdom, I will collect here?

What are my repeated symbols in my dreams?

_____

_____

_____

_____

_____

_____

_____

_____

_____

_____

_____

_____

_____

_____

What would I journal about my dreams?

_____

_____

_____

_____

_____

_____

_____

_____

_____

_____

_____

_____

_____

_____

_____

A pure soul is like a fine pearl. As long as it is hidden in the shell,
at the bottom of the sea, no one thinks of admiring it.
But if you bring it into the sunshine,
this pearl will shine and attract all eyes.
Thus the pure soul, which is hidden from the eyes of the world,
will one day shine before the Angels in the sunshine of eternity.
—John Vianney

Chapter 14

DISCOVER YOUR TALENTS AND RELEASE PAIN THROUGH PAST LIFE REGRESSION

Have you ever asked yourself how come some people are talented in one artistic pursuit or another, such as dancing, painting, or music, since childhood? How did they learn at that young age and perform at such a high level at that young age? "Some children are talented"—I've heard that answer. Remember in chapter 6, you had a practice wherein you listed your talents in this lifetime? Have you noticed if they came from your ancestors? Your parents? Some talents came from our ancestors, our grandmothers and grandfathers, or our parents. What talents did your parents have? What did they pass on to you? Or maybe they came from your soul and your past lives.

I was interested in that question for a while. I purchased the audio book called *Eternal Return* by Roger Woolger, a Jungian analyst, and dove into his stories and meditations and exploration about this particular topic. Roger Woolger used the Active Imagination (Jungian term). He did not use hypnosis, as is usually done for any type of regression: Past Life Regression or Future Life Progression.

Discover Your Past-Life Talents

My first exploration of Past Life Regressions began during one rainy February evening in my Los Angeles home. I lit a candle, silenced my cell phone, and turned on his meditation. His voice started to create a light meditative state by taking me to my childhood memories and, specifically, childhood games. It guided me to the questions "Whom did I like to play with? What toys did I like? What games did I play?"

My memories started to slide into my early childhood, when I had dolls. I liked to play with them by dressing them and changing many different clothes, and specifically, I liked to imagine I would create new clothes or different variations of clothes.

Slowly, his voice guided me to a deeper state of trance, and the next image that surfaced to my awareness was a young woman looking at different types of beautiful fabric and buying it at a market from a merchant, seemingly a European village market, maybe around the eighteenth century.

I was able to identify myself as a young woman. I was observing as if I were part of a movie, buying the beautiful fabric with different textures and colors and seeing myself coming back home, where I already had a female customer waiting for me at the door.

When you experience a Past Life Regression process, you will be guided by the therapist from one scene to another to identify the pain moments of that lifetime, a turning point, or a conflict that needs to be released. In order to get healing from past-life experiences, we usually collect the learnings and release the negative energy of the conflict. This time around, I was looking for a resourceful past life, exploring my talents through childhood games.

In the next scene, I saw myself in a spacious room with a big mirror, in simple attire. I was helping to dress a noble, beautiful woman who'd come to me to finalize the details and fit on her customized dress. That was my passion in that lifetime.

I enjoyed producing beautiful outfits and making women look astonishing in that lifetime and was enjoying the process. I didn't have a husband or children. I was mesmerized by and immersed in the creation process. I was just exploring the art of creation and making women happy. This was my exciting, creative lifetime.

Interestingly enough, in this lifetime, when I was in my early teenage years, my teacher noticed that sewing came easily to me, and she suggested I go to designers' school.

She had a colleague there, and I was accepted to that designer school of making clothes. I enjoyed it. Creating the clothes was so easy and effortless I started to make clothes for myself, my mom, and my friends.

When I was twenty, I was selling my apparel at boutiques. The process of making designer clothes was easy and enjoyable for me. I could make a business suit or an evening dress in a couple of days from scratch. It was so mesmerizing and satisfying that it felt like one song during that creation process; time no longer existed, and I was one with my creation. As if I were in a trance, I did not know where the knowledge or designer ideas came from, as if I channeled them. It was easy and effortless. My girlfriends stood in line to get their uniquely designed dresses, jackets, or suits—one of a kind. My creativity, experience, and passion from my past life were paying off.

It was a great time of enjoyment, fun, and satisfaction. During this passionate, energizing process, I didn't even know how my hands were moving. They were moving by themselves, as if memories from that past life were streaming down, creating it, not me. I was experiencing a creative trance when I was doing it.

When people would ask, "How did you do it?" I would not be able to describe it. It just happened.

Where did this talent and gift come from? No one in my family, not even my grandmothers, had that skill. Did this come from a past life? Or from further down ancestry? My grandmother did not have any knowledge about it. Maybe, they say, mastery comes from experience, and in particular, ten thousand hours is a magic number. Maybe we do have the memories, and mastery comes from our past-life memories.

> Miniexercise: Reflect on what you are good at. What are your talents? Do you think they may come from your previous incarnation? Jot down your thoughts at the end of this chapter.

The other fascinating thing was my yearning to ride a horse. I loved doing it. I never had a fear of riding a horse. I've heard many stories from other people that they are afraid to ride horses or never had a desire to be around them. Some people are like me: they love horses and have a wild desire to have them, ride them, and communicate with them. There is even equestrian therapy in California and other states, wherein people have reparative experiences through communication with horses. Since teenage years, I have had a profound connection to horses as well. I took lessons at the local hippodrome and later took a mountain trip for twelve days on horses in the wilderness. Many years later, I did many Past Life Regressions and found out that riding a horse in my previous incarnations was one of my passions, and I had so much experience with riding horses in my past lives that I did not have any doubt about it in this lifetime.

> Miniexercise: What are your passions? What comes so easily and naturally to you in this lifetime that you do not even have to think about it? Is it playing music? Dancing? Cooking? Driving a car? Sailing a boat? Jot down your aha moments at the end of this chapter, and treasure them as your pearls.

Therapeutic Uses of Past-Life Regression

Many clients and people want to explore their fears and pains or difficult relationships in this lifetime besides their talents or relationships, and many other life challenges can be alleviated through this modality.

To improve my skills, a few years later, I trained in New York with Dr. Brian L. Weiss, MD, who wrote many books on his experience with his clients' Past Life Regressions and how this modality could help to alleviate our challenges and internal conflicts (see the additional resources).

Releasing the Fear of Water

In one popular case presented when I studied at the College of Hypnotherapy, a client was able to release unexplainable fears of water when the wife brought her husband to a hypnotherapist to help him with fear of water.

They could not go on vacation near the ocean or have fun and swim in the pool. He would avoid any kind of body of water. He did not have conscious recollection of trauma in his childhood, and his parents could not recall anything strange that would have created this fear. Nothing was able to help him with regular therapy. When the hypnotherapist regressed him into a previous traumatic life experience, the client saw himself making out with his teenage girlfriend in a car, and the car rolled over into a lake; they both drowned and could not get out of the car.

After just a few sessions, the wife called the therapist and said, "What have you done with my husband?" The therapist anticipated that something bad would follow, but the wife continued. "My husband is buying a house with a pool and getting us a hotel booked by the ocean. I can't believe it!" Wow, what a transformation!

Releasing Panic Attacks and Creating a Free, Happy Life

One of my clients had panic attacks and anxiety. He was on medication that did not work well for him. He wanted to find a way to release his mental and emotional challenges he'd had since teenage time. When I regressed him, he saw himself on a boat in ancient times. The wooden boat experienced a fire, and people were drowning in the middle of the night. He survived, but he felt guilty that he could not save all of the others. During the regression session, he was able to release this "ancient" guilt and anxiety. He saw himself living through his life till the last day with much ease in that ancient lifetime. He felt much better and liberated after that session.

We also created a positive anchor by using lavender oil and finger configuration (the anchoring technique used in hypnotherapy). Seven months later, he called me and shared that he did not have any more panic attacks, and he was able to manage his anxiety with lavender essential oil. He now walks up and down stairs without having a panic attack. The ancient guilt had disappeared in that starry dark sky. It created space for freedom and choice, more conscious awareness, a sense of renewal, and a new story, rather than the old one that no longer served him anymore. He was ready to move on, and later, he moved to a different state and created a new free, happy life.

People are able to create miracles in their lives by exploring their deeper selves through dreams and Past Life Regressions—whoever is ready for their depth exploration and to answer deeper questions and find peace and healing.

Transformational Practices

Technique

In this practice, you may ask yourself these questions: What were your childhood games? Whom did you like to play with? What toys did you use? You may journal your thoughts while asking these questions. See what may come up for you. Keep curiosity high for deeper work. To get the free meditation "Access to Past Life through Childhood Games" (scan QR Code at the end of the book).

My Insights

What did I learn from the story and this exercise? What are my lessons, my pearls of wisdom, I will collect here?

What were my aha moments?

_____

_____

_____

_____

_____

_____

_____

_____

_____

_____

_____

_____

_____

_____

_____

_____

What will I do differently next time?

_____

_____

_____

_____

_____

_____

_____

_____

_____

_____

_____

_____

_____

_____

_____

_____

Who looks outside dreams; who looks inside awakes.
—C. G. Jung

To see a World in a Grain of Sand
And a Heaven in a Wild Flower,
Hold infinity in the palm of your hand
And Eternity in an hour.
—William Blake

Chapter 15

POSSIBILITIES TO FIND DEEPER ANSWERS AND YOUR BLISS

Expansion of Consciousness and Precious Pearl from India

After I landed in India, I went through passport control. Everything was quiet, nice, and cool, like in a muted movie. The moment I came out the outside door, I saw a cheering crowd of people. They were loud and hectic, unlike the quietness inside. What a contrast, like the country itself: India is a country of contrasts. Whoever has been there knows what I mean.

I thanked divinity because with the best luck, I was able to find my taxi driver, Narendra, who took me to his car while ten other taxi drivers followed us, trying to take my suitcase and put it in their cars in the hope that I'd ride with them, not even knowing or caring where I needed to go. It was the beginning of my trip to India.

We drove for about an hour and a half to the yoga center, the place where I was supposed to stay for a few weeks. I had come there to learn a sacred temple dance called Mandala. The retreat was held at the center, where, after our classes were over, we had a choice to participate in a meditation class conducted by a local meditation teacher. Two of my other girlfriends invited me to join them one day. I agreed and came upstairs to experience the class.

The meditation cushions were placed in a circle. We took the empty seats and began the process. He guided us to the seven-chakras meditation created by Osho, an Indian mystic.

At the end of meditation, when we got to the seventh chakra, the crown chakra, he asked us a single question from time to time: "Who are you?" We continued to meditate on the chakra and the nature of the question as well. Time seemed to have disappeared, and only the question stayed in my mind—*Who are you?*—over and over again. It was an eternal, blissful state with no time and no space, just me. By the time I opened my eyes, everybody had left besides me and one other girl. While we were packing up our yoga mats, a conversation started about the impacts and insights we got from meditation.

While the interaction continued, I was watching a mesmerizing sunset from the second floor of the meditation center, which had no windows. Since it was all open, I was able to sense the breeze on my face, with the golden light of the final minutes of the summer evening sunlight. It was surreal and seemed like I was in both worlds: eternal and endless inside and corporeal and finite outside. It all reminded me of that space where I'd met my grandmother during shamanic journeys years ago, where there was no time to be excited. It was pure bliss. Suddenly, the meditation guide asked me again, "So who are you?"

At that same moment, the last glow of the sun was about to disappear. I had a spark in my mind: "Consciousness! I am consciousness! I am this sun, I am this room, I am this body, I am meditation, and I am this ocean. I am sunset, dawn, and starry night." I was mesmerized by the beauty and clarity I suddenly had. It was blissful. It was so clear, like I would see images while doing Holotropic Breathwork™, wherein I would feel that water had its own consciousness. It's the same way you feel profound connection with everything around you. Oneness! Everything has its one eye, and it communicates with you on a profound level. Like *namaste*'s meaning: "I honor the place in you in which the entire universe dwells. I honor the place in you that is of love, of truth, of light, and of peace. When you are in that place in you and I am in that place in me, we are one!"

Prior to this awakening, I had seen downloads of visions of my past lives being reincarnated in India, studying scripts, doing pujas in temples, wearing a sari, and reading Sanskrit. These images were presented to me in almost every meditation we had daily before closing our training day.

This was magical. I felt I'd seen it before. I had lived there before. I had been walking on those streets, seeing walking cows (sacred animals in India) and local people. Every sunset, sunrise, and fruit felt like a long-forgotten memory coming back, feeling intimately familiar. Some insights were deep, reminding me of the connection with this culture; its philosophy; and the ancient temples, buildings, decorations on the walls, scriptures, and nature.

A few days after this experience, I flew back to Los Angeles, where I also felt at home, the same but different. I had lived there for more than a decade by then. Welcomed home by an LAX customs agent, I stepped out of the airport, and rainy December met me outside the airport. I was filled with insights, love, and grace from that trip. I still had an expanded state of consciousness, as can be produced by a deep meditative state. Even though I was on the other side of the globe, I was still feeling the taste of turmeric, anise, and other spices and incense I'd felt on every corner in India.

Unfortunately or fortunately, I had an unusual jet lag for almost two weeks this time. I was up the whole night and sleepy during the day. The wall of rain during January was helpful to meditate during nighttime for five to six hours with prerecorded meditations on Kashmir Shaivism by Sally Kempton.

After almost two weeks of continually meditating every night, I was able to make my way back to a Western lifestyle. One day I felt a sudden opening again, and I reread *The Cosmic Game* by Stan Grof in just a couple of days. This book gave me a description and language for my experiences. It brought a new dimension of understanding and integrating my previous experiences from India, meditating during rainy nights, and recollecting the experiences of oneness I was familiar with during Holotropic Breathwork™. I had the profound experience of being able to relive these insights. That state of Oneness and Consciousness of Bliss is described in Kashmir Saivism's sacred texts. That state I could experience over and over again, yet it slips away when you are diving into regular, mundane tasks of the Western lifestyle. There is no space for it in your daily life, as I thought. I was searching for the state where I could keep this perspective of deep awakening and live life in every moment. That was my precious gift, my pearl, from India.

Deep Regressed Hypnotic Session to Explore Deeper Questions

I scheduled a Life Between Lives session (developed by Michael Newton, PhD), hoping to get answers from my spiritual guides and teachers, counsel of wise ones. I asked them, "How can I keep this 'soul perspective' [my term], an expanded state of consciousness, during mundane daily life?"

"It's hard, but you can do it," I heard.

During this hypnotic session, I was feeling free, seeing the circle of counsel, seeing life from the soul perspective, coming back with new insights, and learning how to live life with new perspective and new aha moments.

As a result, I created the capacity to build new relationships and have a deep, profound compassion for people who are on the way of growth and development on the same journey. The stage in the transformational process, in alchemical terms, is called rubedo, or reddening, wherein you learn how to live your insight, new perspectives, and a new expanded state of consciousness.

How to Keep Your Bliss: Is It Possible to Be Always in This Blissful State?

Once, Sally Kempton shared a story in her class that made a great impact on my search for that blissful state to live in constantly. She shared that sages were asked the same question: "How do you live your bliss constantly, and is it possible at all?" One explained that he was sliding back to the human state of physicality and experiencing emotions with an ordinary state of consciousness but said, "I know how to get back home—to that Oneness." Wow! What an answer!

Consistent meditation practice is necessary. The more you meditate or systematically have spiritual practice, the more you are able to create a space of silence in your mind. In silence, wisdom emerges, and you will be able to feel that true nature that can be felt right after your meditation.

The more you meditate, the more you create that window of peace and silence, the afterglow of meditation. That can fill the space in between your thoughts, which will open up the profound

and unconditional, limitless true love that is your true nature to the depth of your being. You're able to bring back not only from the depths but also from the heights of your expanded state of consciousness the pearls of wisdom, to be fully aware of them and share their preciousness with other human beings.

Practicing the Blissful States

To keep coming back to that blissful state and remind myself of these glimpses of these eternal states, besides doing regular meditation and other spiritual practices, I found it very helpful to listen to a mantra song, which created the biggest impression on me, feeling like coming "back home" to reunite with my true nature.

It is "The Shiva Song." "I am consciousness-bliss. I am Shiva (Chidananda Rupa Shivoham Shivoham)," Deva Premal sings. It's a mesmerizing musical composition. You may find it on YouTube (https://www.youtube.com/watch?v=r5Ca-VIzQH0). Adi Shankara, of the eighth century, summarized the entirety of Advaita Vedanta in six stanzas. These stanzas are known as "Atma Shatakam."

In essence, it is deconstructing our illusions about reality: the roles we may associate ourselves with; the story of our lives that may start to define us; visual, sensational experiences; aversions and desires; fears; mantras; and thoughts. It says, "I'm none of that. I'm everything. I am everywhere. I am consciousness. I am bliss!"

It reminds me of a similar philosophical concept of Tao, or Dao (the Way), which is used in philosophical Taoism. Tao is not a name for an object but an underlying principle of the universe.

What are your deep searches for the true nature? What are your pearls? Journal on the next page your experiences and impressions.

Transformational Practices

Technique

Ask yourself, "Who am I? What is my true nature?" Jot down your impressions and reflections below or in your journal.

My Insights

What did I learn from the story and this exercise? What are my lessons, my pearls of wisdom, I will collect here?

What were my aha moments?

_____

_____

_____

_____

_____

_____

_____

_____

_____

_____

_____

_____

_____

_____

_____

_____

Who am I? What is my true nature?

_____

_____

_____

_____

_____

_____

_____

_____

_____

_____

_____

_____

_____

_____

_____

_____

My joy is like spring, so warm it makes
flowers bloom in all walks of life.
My pain is like a river of tears, so full it fills the four oceans.
Please call me by my true names,
so I can hear all my cries and laughs at once,
so I can see that my joy and pain are one.
Please call me by my true names,
so I can wake up,
and so the door of my heart can be left open,
the door of compassion.
—Thich Nhat Hanh

Chapter 16

ENJOY YOUR FREEDOM AND WHOLENESS THROUGH HOLOTROPIC BREATHWORK™

My trip to India created a great and amazing shift in my consciousness. I was still integrating it months and months afterward while living my ordinary Western life. *Oneness, Consciousness, Cosmic Game, Lila*—those concepts were penetrating my thoughts every day.

I pulled out my mandala drawings, which are usually part of the integration process after the Holotropic Breathwork™ sessions. One of those mandalas reminded me of a painting of Alex Gray, a visionary artist. I saw his paintings much later, after I had created that mandala, knowing it did not come from his work. As C. G. Jung would say, it comes from the Unconscious. I drew eyes "looking at me from everywhere"—from the droplets of the ocean, from the eyes of a deer, from the sky and the stars. The divine intelligence is "looking at you" as part of you, reminding you about your true nature and expanded

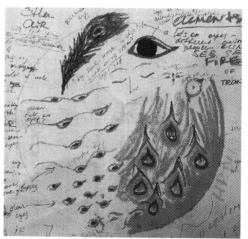

state of consciousness. I saw the intelligence in the dewdrop and felt a connection with an entire ocean and the animals, the mother's womb, and the cosmos. It was as if we were all thriving to wholeness, oneness, and unconditional love. That was my visual anchor of the depth of experiences I was able to carry with me to the surface of my consciousness and life.

What Is Holotropic Breathwork™?

Holotropic, in Greek, means "moving toward wholeness." That is the ultimate goal for us, isn't it? It is to become whole, healed, and complete.

Holotropic Breathwork™ is an amazing, healing, therapeutic modality, which was created by Dr. Stan and Kristina Grof, offers our psyche to journey through realms of our conscious and unconscious, collective conscious, and unconscious material through special settings and type of breathing accompanied by music and facilitators. There is a whole range of experiences you can have during breathwork sessions: body healing, blissful experiences, sorrow, deep grief, rage, or unconditional love. It depends how much healing a person has done and how many layers have been uncovered.

With this modality, you may bring back to the conscious level the pearls of wisdom: the insights, healing, peace, love, and completion.

After experiencing expanded, nonordinary, altered states of consciousness, you need to integrate those deep experiences into your daily life to upgrade your operating system so you can function more efficiently and connect with and relate to people and yourself through love, not through pain. It is a gift to be able to pay attention, be aware of the truth and love, and enjoy life. Every moment you may have missed before becomes precious and cherished.

My Early Experiences with Holotropic Breathwork™

Familiarity with this breathwork modality began when I was in my teens. For the first five sessions, I experienced an oceanic state of being and floating in the cosmos, as if I were floating in my mother's womb, the good womb that was nourishing and warm, where all my needs were taken care of. This is called the first Basic Perinatal Matrix, developed by Dr. Stan Grof, MD. According to Grof, when a child is born, it goes through four stages. Dr. Stan Grof coined the term *Basic Perinatal Matrices* (BPMs). The first stage is a beautiful, amazing, all-loving state. The second is when the contractions start happening, but the cervix is not opened yet, and pressure on the fetus is strong; it feels like it has been almost smashed. It's a feeling of inescapable death. The third stage is when the cervix is opening up, and the child is going through the tunnel, fighting for its life. The fourth one is liberation, when the child is out of the womb and gets into the light.

These four stages of birth can be re-experienced when you are an adult during breathwork sessions in "nonordinary" states of consciousness (Stan Grof's term). The body remembers what happens during birth through implicit memory. If there was any trauma or complication, then the body brings it out during the process when the person is ready. The inner healer (inner wise intelligence) knows when the person is ready to process any kind of trauma, even from the past life. The liberation state and the all-loving state after pushing against pillows that imitate the pressure of pushing through the birth canal (during the workshop, facilitators provide you with help to assist you with whatever is needed to facilitate the process) were great states of rebirth. Powerful, ecstatic music supports you during all four stages of the journey and birthing process: from trance-inducing music to breakthrough music, heart music, and meditative music. To close the session, music takes you on your journey with this spaciousness and the ambiance of dolphin sounds. It is a powerful process and tool to facilitate transformative experiences. I've seen many breakthroughs during these Holotropic Breathwork™ workshops.

Gaining New Perspective and Peeling Even Deeper Layers with Holotropic Breathwork Sessions

During these transformative seminars, people get healing and insight about their lives, their relationships, and the meaning of their lives. It is profound for most of the participants.

One of my recent breathwork sessions was able to help me release the grip of "making life happen" rather than observing, having it flow through me (like Tao), being in the flow, and trusting the process of life. During this weeklong retreat, we had a group of twenty people settle down on individual mats, getting ready for our journeys to the depths again to retrieve our wisdom and healing. Most of the participants this time around were experienced divers into the psyche—as Dr. Stan Grof says, "psychonauts."

The facilitator gave us the last instructions about breathing, and we were ready to embark on the journey. The drumming started, and the music slowly picked up speed and intensity, from slow and low to gradually more and more intense and rhythmic. The breath, with full belly rising and dropping, with intense breath in and out without pause in between, was filling up the body with more oxygen and life force and being one with that music and movement.

Everything disappeared: the room, the facilitators, and the other participants. There were just body movements, music, and breath. Brazilian Amazonian nature sounds and drumming filled up the whole space and swept me away beyond that room and time.

While the body is in the room and the psyche is traveling all the way far away in different realms, movements pick up speed and amplitude, and you become one with the sounds of the other participants and great music. The body is moving through the different rhythms and keeping it going. There are no thoughts or past recollection; you can just be. Be one with yourself, music, rhythm, and life itself, getting into the rhythm of life and seeing the life force moving through you the same way life force moves through a river, the ocean, or the roots of a great tree. Sacred Oneness.

It's like seeing the magnificence of a redwood tree or a sequoia that lived through the Ice Age, seeing the metamorphosis of all living creatures on earth, being in the flow of wind, and moving toward the starry night sky all at the same time, being simultaneously everywhere at each corner of the universe and creation in general. As "The Song of Shiva" says, "I am consciousness. I am bliss!" (see the resources).

You know the phrase: the macrocosm resembles the microcosm, and vice versa. As above, so below. Feeling this deep, profound connection to the intelligence inside you and outside the stars and the constellations of the galaxies, feeling that you are the one, thriving, and feeling gratitude toward creation and the Creator. You're feeling this grace and unconditional love and, at the same time, losing track of time.

You're in the space that holds you; and all questions are answered, all problems are solved, and all relationships are healed and harmonized. This is how ecstatic transpersonal experiences can be experienced during sessions of Holotropic Breathwork™ workshops: "I'm one with everything. I am everything!" You are merging with universal consciousness yet maintaining a separate identity. What a journey. When I came back to the room, I saw myself lying down on the mat among other participants.

We all went through individual journeys and were happy to come back to our bodies, to the room, and to an ordinary state of consciousness, bringing wisdom and expansiveness to our lives.

Trees Do Not Grieve Their Fallen Leaves

Usually, my breathwork experience is deep and profound. In contrast, my last breathwork session was totally different from all the other ones. That time around, I was triggered by the sounds of the other participants going through their own healing processes and not so much quiet but intense screaming and movement. My chatty mind kicked in and started to wander, thinking about what happened in my life and whatnot, remembering past breakthrough sessions in breathwork, and being aggravated by the sounds people around me made.

Suddenly, I realized my pain came from making life happen again, rather than being at peace with what was. I started to breathe even more intensely, so the breath, as a vehicle of the process, took me even deeper, rather than staying on the surface of the conscious level and listening to the endless stories of a rational mind. Diving deeper into your subconscious mind, you touch something that otherwise cannot pass through the suppression and defense mechanisms of the mind; you dive deeper into suppressed truth or pain. It was another layer of consciousness I was exploring again.

We never know what the wisdom of the inner healer will bring to work through. As Dr. Stan Grof says, "Let your breath surprise you." Your inner healer, your inner wisdom, knows what you are ready for today to heal.

That day, I was going through deep pain that took me again through the past memories of people, things, events, and the expectations in life.

All the significant people in my life passed through my inner vision. I saw them as actors playing roles and taking on roles to provide painful experiences and joyful ones. The essence was still the same: soul. I saw them as if all the actors were made from one essence, the same life force.

Then the 4D picture of the actors moved into the image of a tree that represented the life force that streams through all of us, the divine intelligence. That life force is constantly moving and changing; it never stops. It's only we who hold in our minds or try to get attached to pleasure and avoid pain.

This is our human nature. When we are diving into the depths of our being and connecting with divine essence, we are moving from surviving to thriving with increased awareness and compassion. I've experienced a big range of experiences and witnessed others as well, but the one thing I've noticed is the connection with deeper truth and self is making people more compassionate, with more wisdom and acceptance. People who do this type of breathwork feel lighter; look younger; and are more loving, open, and alive.

While integrating my experiences after the last breathwork session, I was sitting and watching the trees let their leaves fall to the ground and watching the wind play with the leaves. A sudden realization came to me: trees do not grieve the fallen leaves; rather, we humans are grasping to the flow of life from the past and creating plans for the future that may never happen. The biggest aha moment came after the breathwork session itself, during integration.

The teaching that came from mindful observation and integration was profound: to be at peace with "what is," to just be, not trying to make life happen. Like Universal Tao. Like Oneness. Bliss.

All experiences are included in the tapestry of life; the fullness of life force moving through you is the same life force moving through the trees and animals, through all of us.

I had seen this ever-changing, simmering tapestry of life and the opposite experiences it brings: integrating the dualities of our world; thus, it can teach you to bring compassion to yourself and others. The leaves swirling in the air are seemingly separated from that branch of the tree, having that seemingly autonomous experience, becoming part of the floating river, and being integrated back to earth to become part of the soil. It's an endless circling of life-force energy and transformation. Endless transformation never stops. In the end, leaves are never apart from that branch and the tree.

I was getting words surfacing in my memory of a poem of a Buddhist Vietnamese monk. It talks about that same ever-changing life force moving through everything and everyone and about living connected to and feeling compassion for all beings. It's Thich Nhat Hanh's "Please Call Me by My True Names": "Please call me by my true names, so I can wake up, and so the door of my heart can be left open, the door of compassion."

Transformational Practices

Technique

Have you ever heard about Holotropic Breathwork™? Have you ever done it? Are you curious about this modality? If you've had experiences, jot them down below. If not, you may search the internet to find a certified practitioner. I list the books of Dr. Stan Grof in the resources.

My Insights

What did I learn from the story and this exercise? What are my lessons, my pearls of wisdom, I will collect here?

_____

_____

_____

_____

_____

_____

_____

_____

_____

_____

What were my aha moments?

_____

_____

_____

_____

_____

_____

_____

_____

_____

_____

_____

_____

_____

What transformational practices have I experienced, including the breathwork?

_____

_____

_____

_____

_____

_____

_____

_____

_____

_____

_____

_____

_____

_____

_____

Follow your bliss.
—J. Campbell

Synchronicity is an ever present reality
for those who have eyes to see.
—C. G. Jung

Chapter 17

HOW DO I KNOW I AM ON THE RIGHT PATH? SYNCHRONICITIES

Meaningful Coincidence?

On a beautiful summer evening last year in the middle of July, I was walking around a Barnes and Noble store, passing by the stands of books. I was just wandering around in the store, not looking for any specific book or anything else. My attention was attracted to a bright yellow book standing on a shelf on the level of my eyes. I reached out my hand to this book, and suddenly, something dropped onto my head and then onto the floor. I picked up the book from the floor and opened it to a random page. The heading was "Show Up and Shine." It was Rebecca Campbell's *Light Is the New Black*, a guide to answering your soul callings and working your light. I continued to read: "Dare to follow your highest calling. Let the message in your heart come flooding out." I found it interesting that this book had fallen onto my head. I'd heard many stories about books falling on people's heads out of nowhere or seen it in movies, but never had a book fallen off a shelf like that before for me. It was intriguing. Laughing inside and wondering what the message was, I went to the cashier. Later, I found out the author of that book was a successful writer and was published by Hay House.

At that time, I had my chapter "Healing the Family Wounds" already submitted to Journey of Riches for editing. It was my first collaboration project with John Spender. The book is called *Transform*

Your Wounds into Wisdom. It was published at the end of October 2022 and became Amazon's number-one international best seller in five countries.

By then, I did not have the manuscript ready for the whole book to be published on my own, even though the book had incubated in me for a few years already. I did not know anything about the book business or book publishing until the collaboration with John. So I bought two books: the yellow one, *Trust Your Vibes* by Sonia Choquette, and the one that had fallen on my head, *Light Is the New Black* by Rebecca Campbell. I happily came back home, desiring to understand the messages from both of these authors.

The following morning, I was checking my email, and I had an email from Balboa Press (which is a division of Hay House, as I found out later) with a number of options to publish a book. I was amazed and thrilled by these incredible coincidences. Here I am, submitting my manuscript to Balboa Press.

Later on, I realized I had Rebecca Campbell's Rose Oracle cards, which I'd purchased a couple of months before her book fell onto my head. Only after getting the email from Balboa Press did I start to see where it all was going. What a coincidence! Finally, I've gotten the message, universe! Thank you!

A lot of my clients ask, while going through changes, "How do I know I am on the right track?" What an interesting question. Have you asked yourself this question before? I did. I asked this question many times. In my search and deep work I have done, I have been given an answer: synchronicities.

What are the synchronicities?

C. G. Jung and Synchronicity

The term *synchronicity* was initially coined by C. G. Jung, a Swiss psychiatrist. It refers to meaningful coincidences. He observed many instances in his own life and his private practice while working with patients. He wrote about this phenomenon in his work in *Synchronicity: An Acausal*

Connecting Principle, published in 1960. He described a famous story about a patient who shared a dream in a therapy session, wherein she was given a golden scarab. The moment the client shared the dream symbol, Jung heard something by the window. He went to see what it was and found that a beetle similar to a scarab was trying to get inside. He opened the window and showed it to his client. This synchronistic event created such an impact on her course of therapy that she had a major breakthrough after that.

Another great example of extraordinary coincidence I experienced myself. This happened when I again encountered magical, meaningful coincidence.

Synchronicities and Humor of the Goddess

It happened after my last holotropic session during the six-day module. I finished creating my mandala and a collage to integrate the amazing, extraordinary experiences. I brought my attention to the Goddess Oracle, which was sitting on the table next to the painting materials, and pulled out the card. The name was Gyhldeptis, the forest goddess of the Tlingit and Haida people of North America. The meaning of the card was "Gyhldeptis glides into your life to tell you the way to wholeness for you now lies in synthesis. It's time to bring in all the divergent parts, all the opposing pieces, together into one whole you" (*The Oracle Goddess*, 73).

I was following the ritual suggestion, where you travel down a tunnel to meet this goddess and have a feast at her Festival House, where the goddess brings the feast in your honor. When I looked at the table, the other seats were served with plates as well and were empty, as if she were expecting someone else. I asked her about other guests, and she said, "The empty seats are for the other pieces of you."

I invited all the pieces that needed to be integrated into the wholeness and seated them at the table, so all the parts would be "fed" what they needed at that time, so they could be part of me and be honored and acknowledged and later synthesized into me to create a powerful, resilient, magnificent, whole me.

All parts of myself presented themselves. The parts were delighted to satisfy their needs. The Inner Child wanted to be protected; another part desired to be fed with the sweetness of life. The other parts voiced their needs and wants as well. Once all the parts' desires were fulfilled, each and every one of them was integrated into me.

I felt so much energy, completeness, and power, like when we evoke resourceful states and anchor them with the Ring of Power described in part 2. The same surge of energy was going through my body, my essence, my being. It was even more powerful because after breathwork, a person is in such a vulnerable, susceptible, gentle state, and the integration process takes some time to be fully anchored in the body.

The magic happened when I finished my meditation and opened my eyes. The other female participant sat next to me and placed a dessert plate with a few pieces of chocolate for me, offering the "sweetness" of life with a welcoming smile. I was touched by these synchronicities again and by the humor of the universe, the divine intelligence, and the goddess. I knew it was a gift from a goddess with humor: one of my parts was looking for something sweet, and it literally appeared in front of me the moment I came back to the ordinary world from my meditation. I thanked both the goddess internally and the person externally who offered me chocolate, enjoying the sweetness of chocolate, life, and synchronicities again and again.

How to Work with Them

I have noticed that the more you do spiritual practice, the more you get these meaningful coincidences, especially when the universe starts to show a great sense of humor. Pay attention, and observe synchronicities, collecting them and making notes. I see them in my practice with clients all the time. Here is one of the beautiful examples.

Carrie had her hope ignited by the progress she was making. She came to one of her following sessions for coaching to achieve her goals, and specifically, she wanted to manifest her long-lasting dream of flying over Rio. For her, the dream was vivid, but she could not imagine that it could really happen. During the beginning phase of her breakthrough coaching, she came to a session and shared, "I was driving my car the other day, and a song came on the radio: 'I believe I can fly. I believe I can touch the sky.' I started to cry because I could not believe it. I realized I did not believe in myself."

I mentioned to her that synchronicities were starting to occur in her life. According to C. G. Jung, we are on the right path when such a process happens to us. Synchronicities can happen anytime, and we have to be open to them. For example, you could hear the answer to your question from someone standing next to you in line or, as Carrie did, on the radio. Be aware, and pay attention. The universe is always talking to us with signs and symbols in our dreams and meditations as well.

"Do these signs mean I'm on the right track with my mindset?" Carrie asked.

"Exactly," I said.

Carrie finished her breakthrough sessions, and six months later, she sent me a note that she was on her way to Brazil. While I read her note, that song about believing in herself played in my mind like an echo of her hard work and her success she wanted to share with me. This story I share fully in the book called *Master Your Mindset*, in the series Journey of Riches, published in February 2023.

Often in my practice, I find that when clients are working on their problems, solutions are presented in synchronicities, or I will watch a movie about a similar issue that may have a solution or have resonance to their situation. It often comes with a great sense of humor from the universe.

I had another fascinating, humorous coincidence when I was working on my book, specifically on the image of the cover of my book. I was listening to a Ted Talk on YouTube by Chip Kidd about how to create or find a cover for your book. He gave the example during his Ted Talk of how he created the logo for Jurassic Park. The next day, I was passing by the Museum of Science, where they had a dinosaur exhibition. I laughed; the universe was "winking" at me. You cannot make this up.

These messages may show up when you are on the right path for manifesting heartfelt desires or in your healing journey. The more you pay attention to them, remember them, and collect them, the more you will feel strong and firm in your belief that you are moving in the right direction.

Enjoy these meaningful coincidences, and have fun! Know that you are on the right path. Good luck!

Transformational Practices

Technique

Ask yourself, "Have I ever paid attention to or remembered the meaningful coincidences in my life? Were they amusing or entertaining?" If yes, collect your stories as pearls in your journal. If you have never paid attention to them, start observing them when they show up in your life, and write them down.

My Insights

What did I learn from the story and this exercise? What are my lessons, my pearls of wisdom, I will collect here?

_____

_____

_____

_____

_____

_____

_____

_____

_____

What were my aha moments?

_____

_____

_____

_____

_____

_____

_____

_____

_____

_____

_____

_____

_____

_____

My synchronicities

There is a Secret One inside us;
the planets in all the galaxies
pass through his hands like beads.
That is a string of beads one should look at
with luminous eyes.
—Kabir, fifteenth-century Indian sage

Chapter 18

INTEGRATION: CREATION OF THE SYMBOL OF YOUR JOURNEY

Congratulations! You are finishing this transformational journey and getting to the end of the book after witnessing others' journeys and gaining your own insights, aha moments, and expanded states of consciousness; healing the pains and wounds; and collecting your pearls of wisdom. An important step left on your journey is to integrate these new states into your daily life. I see this over and over again when people pay attention to this important part of the process: when they live through these new choices, taking actions toward their goals, seeing new horizons, and following their heartfelt desires and creative pursuits, they become happier and more joyful and keep those attained resourceful and peak states, so they can live the new and best versions of themselves.

Being on that new level after solving problems, coming out from a crisis, acquiring new resources, having more resilience, knowing yourself better and more deeply, and improving your relationships. In alchemical terms of transformation is a stage called reddening, wherein a new personality, new habits, and new ideas are part of living your new wisdom and renewed sense of self.

Also, remember the Universal Model of Change from chapter 12 and the journey of change from A to A' through the pitfalls of point B to C and upward movement to D? Once new events happen, a new level after A' may become point B and then drop to C again. Remember that is an opportunity for you to dive in even deeper, peel more layers, and retrieve your pearls of wisdom. It's your opportunity to journey again and be on your heroic path every day. Be an example to others, showing that an elevated mindset and a joyful life are possible. Yes, it's time to live with an expanded state of consciousness after the pain of a contracted state of consciousness. Now it's time to live your new level of development.

As you may already know, healing is to become whole and complete. Let me share with you great words from *The Goddess Oracle*: "Wholeness is created when all the parts are honored and listened to, when all parts are brought together and synthesized into a whole. The greatest gifts to the whole often lie in the most disparate pieces" (74). Hopefully, you have become more aware of those parts that were forgotten and disowned and now have learned how to bring them together. It's time to integrate them, remember them, and become whole.

How do we treat ourselves? How do we nourish ourselves, literally and symbolically? The metaphor that came up for me during one of the sessions: becoming whole by putting pieces of a pie together one by one. When you finally fill all the pieces, you become whole and complete, the "food" we nourish ourselves with. You add more parts of the pie to yourself, and eventually, it will become whole and complete. Nourishing yourself with "wholesome food" creates this wholeness.

Once you become aware of it and identify the relationships that nourish or poison and give energy or take away energy and deplete, ask yourself, "Does this make me feel good or depleted?"

Why do people continue to poison themselves instead of loving, cherishing, nourishing, and valuing? It pertains similarly to the relationship with food. It is there for us as a substitution for real relationships. It's again to remind you that there is a possibility to work through your human biographical material and also your ancestral roots. There is an opportunity to work also with your emotions, refining your mind.

There is a space that can be created to dive deeper into your soul and psyche through dreams, hypnosis, regressions, and meditations, and you can dive deeper into transpersonal experiences, such as oneness, cosmic creativity, and bliss, with deeper techniques that take you beyond your biographical material into the spiritual realm.

As you have read the stories, you have experienced them and witnessed them, and if you have gone through the journey of exercises, you may have noticed that each exercise after each chapter is designed to help you to gain insight. See the difference when you scroll through the book backward now and read through your journaling and your pearls of wisdom. You may notice great changes that happened to you through this incredible journey. Seek more practice around people and more integration as well. I created an online class where you can learn more and participate in live Q&A weekly sessions, so you can be supported and witnessed in your progress. If you need more information, please visit my website to get access to free meditations and training (see the additional resources).

Different Ways to Integrate Your Insights and Learn to Live Your New Gains

A useful part of integration is sharing your experiences in groups or with your therapist, coach, and trusted friends. **Sharing the experiences** in groups, listening to the stories and sharing them, gives us a feeling of belonging to a tribe. We find acceptance by sharing similar context and transformative material, which "downloads" in the brain and mind the experiences to accelerate the evolution by encoding the successful strategy in mind, expand its understanding about the world around us, and dive deeper internally into the sacred realm. You may talk to a trusted person or therapist to help guide you to process those symbols and maybe work through the emotions. Share in a group or a circle or other safe space where you will be heard, seen, accepted, listened to, and given space for your unique individuality to embrace your world and your pearls of wisdom you are ready to share with others.

You are already familiar with **journaling.** It is helpful to come back and see the progression, themes of the journey that took place, growth, and development to capture the content and create the narrative that can be later shared in a group or with your therapist.

You may **move your body or dance** as a way for the body to release or move your energy through a particular expression. You can dance or move with eyes closed (just make sure it's safe for you to move that way). During a shamanic workshop connected to working with dreams and their symbols with specific techniques, we were invited to dance out our dreams to embody those symbols and have them become part of us. Also, journaling and analyzing dreams are the most usual ways of understanding your subconscious material, as well as using Jungian active imagination technique.

You may choose to **create symbols** that will remind you in daily life of your journey. It could be a **bracelet or necklace** that represents the journey and healing on your sacred, unique path, or you may just collect your pearls in a sacred box.

You also can **draw or paint images** from your dreams, from breathwork, or from a vision board. It is helpful to have diverse painting material. Do finger painting to create a more visceral, sensational experience, or create watercolor, abstract representations of your dream symbols or images.

Collage is another way to integrate insights and learnings, using evocative images that may draw your attention and also represent moments or the whole journey. After placing your collage or painting in the most seen place, you can integrate the images or symbols from your subconscious mind that will help you to live your new version of yourself, new insights, and new behavior.

You may bring out **clay** and play with it with your eyes closed and feel what will come out for you to see what figure will emerge from this space between you and your hands and your subconscious mind. Aren't you curious?

A beautiful and artistic way to integrate into your life is to anchor your experiences by **singing or creating music**. Some people find it helpful as well to express their emotions and unique artistic way of integrating insights and wisdom.

The creation of an **altar** helps me to connect with the symbols of my journey or insightful images. Put pictures on the altar—or deities or crystals—that represent symbolic connections to the unseen realm.

You may also use objects, pictures, flowers, or jewels—whatever makes you dive into that special place in yourself where you feel love, healing, and oneness. The namaste hand gesture in the Vedas is used. It mostly occurs as a salutation to a divinity that dwells in your heart and my heart, and when we are in our heart space, you and I unite and become one in this heart space. What is the symbol of your heart space and heart-to-heart connection? Mine is a beautiful rose quartz heart shape that serves as a reminder of this gentle, loving, caring space.

Collect your pearls any way that is desirable and fulfilling for you. **A bracelet or a necklace as a symbol of your journey** may consist of different-colored beads, with each representing part of your journey that has a connection to the inner world of transformation, serving as its tangible representation.

It will serve you as an anchor, a symbol of what has happened. It may be so meaningful that once you have touched the bracelet, it will take you to the whole story it represents. It will remind you of your sacred journey you once took.

Connecting with and **walking in nature** after these transformative moments on your journey bring rejuvenation. Even after the last breathwork I did, I got incredible, precious insights from nature: I went and sat outside to just be and just breathe, rather than doing things. It was a moment of stillness and grace. I looked at the fallen leaves, with different colors of leaves falling on the ground and being picked up by the wind and thrown onto the river, and the river took them away. Trees do not grieve for fallen leaves. They are at peace with what is, at peace with the process of life. They stay still, rooted in the earth, yet they're alive, able to continue to be rejuvenated in a new season and get new leaves in the spring. Nature always has its wisdom. We just need to pay attention to it and be aware. That was my wisdom gained from the contact with nature. What is yours? Jot down your thoughts at the end of this chapter.

A great reminder is to be gentle with yourself and always give yourself a reward for the courage to go through and face your fears, your shadows. It is a painful yet rewarding transformation that brings you to a next level of living. Give yourself time to integrate this new knowledge and wisdom into your life, as well as new thinking and new behavior.

All of these examples are given for you again to show what resonates with you the most and what is suitable for your unique personality to integrate new pieces of yourself into a more conscious and healed human being. It brings you into wholeness in congruence with your conscious and subconscious minds, your transformed inner hero, and your upgraded operating system, along with installing new applications, to live a fuller, happier, healthier, more joyful life.

Integrative Practices

Technique

Reflect on what kind of practice resonated with you the most. Then choose the best integrative techniques that will serve you at this point in your life, and write them down below. Practice them until you feel you are complete and have fully integrated those particular lessons into your daily life.

My Insights

What did I learn from the story and this exercise? What are my lessons, my pearls of wisdom, I will collect here?

_____

_____

_____

_____

_____

_____

_____

_____

_____

What were my aha moments?

_____

_____

_____

_____

_____

_____

_____

_____

_____

_____

_____

_____

_____

_____

_____

What is the symbol of My Transformational Journey?

_____

_____

_____

_____

_____

_____

_____

_____

_____

_____

_____

_____

_____

_____

Conclusion

Congratulations on ending this particular adventurous, magnificent journey to wholeness with me and my clients' stories. Some of the stories will resonate with you more, and some less. Take the best, and bless the rest! I'm sure you have been able to identify what you would like to work on, haven't you? What would you like to explore more in your life? What would you like to improve? What wisdom would you like to share with others?

These stories described sacred practices coming to light from darkness through doing internal work, cleaning, and shining light through the storms in your life and the shadows we all have. Others went through this, and you too can go through this.

To conclude your journey of exploration of what's possible and what you can do to heal or transform your life, the main idea is to have the goal and a map; be equipped with the right tools; and, if necessary, get a guide for your journey to retrieve your pearls of wisdom, treasure them, and learn from them.

Systematic exploration of transformational practices will allow you to connect your inner light to your true self, making unconscious material conscious and striving toward becoming more whole and complete. Now you know that when you get to an uncomfortable state or hit the ground, this is an opportunity to "dive into exploration" of this challenge, heal from it, and be transformed.

Your goal may be to become the best version of yourself; manifest the life you want; achieve your goals; or heal your relationships with loved ones, family members, and yourself. Or you may need to learn how to give yourself love and care, as a good enough mother would do, or answer fundamental questions for yourself.

After reading and resonating with stories and practicing exercises, you may learn how to live your life after bringing forth your upgraded state of being, with an expanded capacity to love and relate to others, rather than pain or wounds. Realize that a contracted state of consciousness wherein there is only space for pain is an opportunity for growth and improvement.

Know that in life, you will still face difficulties and losses, but you will have the experience encoded in your essence in your memory structure of the journey you have completed. Now you have lived this yourself, and you may show the way to others.

Yes, we are not immune from life, but we now have upgraded tools and mechanisms in our mind to deal with emotional, mental, and relationship difficulties, and we are wiser and more skillful and mature and better able to self-regulate, control, and choose our resourceful states, thoughts, new behavioral patterns, new versions of ourselves, and new types of relations. As Louise Hay said, "You can heal your life" and live a fuller and happier life with richness of relations and emotions.

These stories serve you as a guideline or magical map of a journey that can be taken. The examples enrich you with new powerful, resourceful states and tools with stronger resilience; new perspectives; and a new capacity to love, enjoy life, and relate to a new you and your loved ones.

My clients like the metaphor for a transformational process described as "an upgrade of your software" or installation of a new operational system in your human mind. You're installing new apps and running your human life more efficiently with new strategies, a healed heart, and an elevated mindset, using these soulful, transformational tools.

Feel the freedom; feel this creativity; and feel this bliss of coming out on the other side as renewed, more whole, and at peace with "what is," integrating the opposites of dark and light, transcending the duality of our world, trusting the process of life, and being able to share love and compassion.

Now, after retrieving your insights, your pearls, and journaling your wisdom, you may have already created a symbolic representation of your journey. It may be with beads or pearls or anything else you desire. Maybe wear it on special occasions, or put it in a special box as a symbol of your heroic journey in which you took on earthly life challenges.

And may you take it to the next level: share your knowledge; share your stories; and spread wisdom, love, and learnings to inspire others to heal as well.

Join groups or communities to share your transformational stories. Attend meetups so others are able to witness your sacred journey, and you can witness theirs. Create a community. Spread the elevated state of consciousness, love, connection, relation, and acceptance, listening to and acknowledging each and every person's story.

Create that resonance and ripple effect with "I see you," which equals "I love you" (remember the movie *Avatar*?). Seeing and hearing each and every voice creates diversity and the inclusion of everyone's unique experiences in life. If you choose to learn deeper transformational techniques, sign up for my online course with weekly live Q&A support and training sessions directly with me at DrOlgaZabora.com, where you can be seen, supported, guided and being able to share your healing and transformational story as well.

Be free, be creative, and be blissful!

Love and blessings,
Dr. Olga Zabora

Acknowledgments

This book would not have come out if I hadn't been supported and divinely guided by inner callings and my love for life and people. I was guided by my psyche, my soul, and my Self and was assisted by my guides and teachers both earthly and spiritual. I acknowledge all my teachers past and present and divine assistance as well.

Deep gratitude to all my clients. Without you, it would not be possible to show others how to heal and transform their precious, unique lives. Thank you dear reader, for trusting the inner calling to create transformation in your life and create a ripple effect for others.

Thank you to my parents, who gave me life and, thus, my opportunity to fulfill my mission during this lifetime.

Thank you to my ancestors, who blazed the trail before me, before all of us, and continued life through generations.

Thank you to everybody who supported me on this adventurous and challenging endeavor, including Balboa Press's editorial and other team members.

With Love,

Dr. Olga Zabora, PsyD

BE FREE, BE CREATIVE, BE BLISSFUL

To receive three free gifts from my website,
DrOlgaZabora.com:
Inner Child Meditation
The Ring of Power Training
Past Life Regression Meditation
Scan your QR code:

About the Author

Dr. Olga Zabora, PsyD
International best-selling author, speaker,
Certified Master NLP Coach, and NLP Trainer's Trainer.

She holds a Doctorate Degree in Clinical Psychology; a Diploma of Clinical Hypnotherapy from HMI; and multiple certifications, including Gestalt Therapy from PGI and Jungian Analytical Psychology from the Jung Institute of Los Angeles. She studied Past Life Regression and Spiritual Regression with Dr. Brian L. Weiss, MD, and trained with Dr. Richard Bandler, co-founder of Neuro-Linguistic Programming.

Dr. Zabora was a collaborating author of *Transform Your Wounds into Wisdom*, which became a number-one Amazon best seller in five countries, published in October 2022. She collaborated on a second book, *Master Your Mindset*, which was published in February 2023 and became an international best seller as well (https://www.amazon.com/author/drolgazabora.com).

Dr. Olga's extensive training both in the United States and outside the country, combined with twenty years of education and experience, allows for forward thinking, advanced knowledge and flexibility, and love for life and allows people to create transformational changes in their lives.

Her far-reaching personal experiences and deep explorations include Jungian therapy; dream analysis; Holotropic Breathwork™

with Dr. Stan Grof, MD; meditation; mindfulness; yoga; philosophical tantra with Sally Kempton; sacred temple Mandala dance in India; and multiple studies about feminine nature and energy from world-renowned professionals.

Certificates from the Optimum Health Institute and the Advanced Nutritional and Integrative Medicine for Mental Health Professionals course, studying shamanism for a few years through Michael Harner's foundation, and other spiritual practices have given her opportunities to integrate her knowledge and utilize it in assisting clients with their life journeys and lasting positive changes.

Her passion lies in helping you to become aware of your own resources by bringing up the best parts of yourself to guide you gently in your transformation into the best and happiest version of yourself.

Currently, Dr. Olga continues publishing her books, offers personal breakthrough NLP coaching programs, and Transformational Journey Online Training with live Q&A sessions on DrOlgaZabora.com. She also teaches classes, and conducts empowering women's retreats, along with sharing her humor, knowledge, and experience with everyone who attends her courses at www.GoddessEvent.com.

www.DrOlgaZabora.com

Resources

Publications

Campbell, Rebecca. *Light Is the New Black*. Hay House, 2015.

Grof, Stan. *The Adventure of Self-Discovery*. Albany: State University of New York Press, 1988.

Grof, Stan. *The Cosmic Game*. Albany: State University of New York Press, 1998.

Grof, Stan. *Healing Our Deepest Wounds: The Holotropic Paradigm Shift*. Stream of Experience Productions, 2012.

Grof, Stan. *Psychology of the Future: Lessons from Modern Consciousness Research*. State University of New York Press, 2000.

Hay, Louise. *You Can Heal Your Life*. Hay House, 1984.

Hellinger, Bert. *Love's Own Truths: Bonding and Balancing in Close Relationships*. Zeig, Tucker & Theisen, 2001.

Jung, Carl G. *Psychology of the Unconscious*. Dover Publications, 2003.

Jung, Carl G. *Synchronicity: An Acausal Connecting Principle*. Princeton, NJ: Princeton University Press, 1960.

Kempton, Sally. *Awakening Shakti: The Transformative Power of the Goddesses of Yoga*. Sounds True, 2013.

Lerner, Mark, and Isha Lerner. *Inner Child Cards: A Fairy Tale Tarot*. Bear & Company, 2001.

Manne, Joy. *Family Constellations: A Practical Guide to Uncovering the Origins of Family Conflict*. North Atlantic Books, 2009.

Marashinsky, Amy Sophia. *The Goddess Oracle*. Stamford: US Games Systems, 2006.

Murphy, Joseph. *The Power of Your Subconscious Mind*. TarcherPerigee, 2009.

Newton, Michael. *Journey of Souls*. Llewellyn Publications, 2010.

Schwartz, Robert. *Your Soul's Plan: Discovering the Real Meaning of the Life You Planned before You Were Born*. North Atlantic Books, 2009.

Shankarananda, Swami. *Consciousness Is Everything: The Yoga of Kashmir Shaivism*. Shaktipat Press, 2003.

von Franz, Marie-Louise. *On Divination and Synchronicity: The Psychology of Meaningful Chance*. Inner City Books, 1980.

Wallis, Christopher D. *Tantra Illuminated*. Mattamayura Press, 2013.

Weiss, Brian L. *Many Lives, Many Masters*. Touchstone, 2012.

Weiss, Brian. *Same Soul, Many Bodies*. FreePress, 2005.

Weiss, Brian L., and Amy E. Weiss. *Miracles Happen: The Transformational Healing Power of Past-Life Memories*. HarperOne, 2013.

Whitmont, Edward C., and Silvia B. Perera. *Dreams: A Portal to the Source*. Routledge, 1991.

Wikman, Monika. *Pregnant Darkness: Alchemy and the Rebirth of Consciousness*. Nicolas-Hays, 2004.

Woolger, Roger. *Other Lives, Other Selves*. Bantam, 1988.

Zabora, Olga. "The Breakthrough with Elevated Mindset." In *Master Your Mindset*. Las Vegas: Motion Media International, 2023.

Zabora, Olga. "Heal Your Family Wounds." In *Transform Your Wounds into Wisdom*. Crawfordsville: Motion Media International, 2022.

Video Resources

Alpha. Movie. 2018.

Grof, Stan. "The Depth of the Psyche." https://www.youtube.com/watch?v=3uCySQOMB-4.

Grof, Stan. "The Holotropic Breathwork." https://www.youtube.com/watch?v=5VcUJjRC-Hc.

Grof, Stan. "Proposal for a Radical Revision of Psychiatry, Psychology, & Psychotherapy." https://www.youtube.com/watch?v=i-aSLt3IKUs.

Il Divo. "Amazing Grace." https://www.youtube.com/watch?v=GYMLM j-SibU.

Joel, Billy. "In the Middle of the Night." https://www.youtube.com/watch?v=fo_vn_Ilsu8.

Past-life regression meditation, inner child meditation, and Ring of Power training. www.DrOlgaZabora.com.

"Song of Shiva." https://www.youtube.com/watch?v=r5Ca-VIzQH0.

Printed in the United States
by Baker & Taylor Publisher Services